Disability Studies in Education

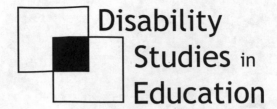

Disability Studies in Education

Susan L. Gabel and Scot Danforth
General Editors

Vol. 3

PETER LANG
New York • Washington, D.C./Baltimore • Bern
Frankfurt am Main • Berlin • Brussels • Vienna • Oxford

Disability Studies in Education

Readings in Theory and Method

editor
Susan L. Gabel

PETER LANG
New York • Washington, D.C./Baltimore • Bern
Frankfurt am Main • Berlin • Brussels • Vienna • Oxford

Library of Congress Cataloging-in-Publication Data

Disability studies in education: readings in theory and method /
edited by Susan L. Gabel.
p. cm. — (Disability studies in education; vol. 3).
Includes bibliographical references and index.
1. People with disabilities—Education. 2. Critical pedagogy.
I. Gabel, Susan L. (Susan Lynn). II. Series.
LC4019.D56   379'.071—dc22   2005005592
ISBN 0-8204-5549-0
ISSN 1548-7210

Bibliographic information published by **Die Deutsche Bibliothek**.
Die Deutsche Bibliothek lists this publication in the "Deutsche
Nationalbibliografie"; detailed bibliographic data is available
on the Internet at http://dnb.ddb.de/.

Cover design by Sophie Boorsch Appel

The paper in this book meets the guidelines for permanence and durability
of the Committee on Production Guidelines for Book Longevity
of the Council of Library Resources.

© 2005 Peter Lang Publishing, Inc., New York
275 Seventh Avenue, 28th Floor, New York, NY 10001
www.peterlangusa.com

Printed in the United States of America

For Peter,
ever faithful, patient, supportive,
stubborn, passionate, and brave

Contents

Acknowledgments

I am grateful to the contributors in this book. They have patiently awaited its publication and I am thankful they all remained committed to the project. Others, whose support and encouragement regarding this and other projects I tackle, include: Pete Gabel, Sandi McClennen, Judith Sheldon, and Anita Ghai. Thanks to Phil Ferguson for his thoughtful review of the book.

Special thanks to the pioneers, some retired and others still "at play in the fields," whose work was sometimes lonely and ridiculed and whose legacies live on in the work of the contributors to this volume. Special thanks to Lous Heshusius, whose scholarly courage is a model for us all.

Finally, my deepest appreciation goes to those who have taught me about disability as a lived experience: Bob, Tiffany, April, Benjamin.

1 Introduction: Disability Studies in Education

Susan Gabel

In spite of the growing influence of disability studies over the last three decades, educational researchers, by and large, have come late to a movement that that began officially with a proclamation by the Union of Physically Impaired Against Segregation (UPIAS) in 1972 in the United Kingdom and with the founding of the Society for Disability Studies (SDS) in the United States in 1982. Since 1990, the Modern Language Association (MLA) and the American Anthropological Association (AAA) have formed special interest or discussion groups for their members. Finally, in 1999, almost thirty years after the UPIAS statement and almost twenty years after the founding of SDS, a special interest group (SIG) of the American Educational Research Association (AERA), "Disability Studies in Education" (DSE), was formed, marking the formal beginning of what has become a growing movement in educational research, theory and practice. The SIG describes disability studies and its application to education as follows.

> Disability studies is an emerging interdisciplinary field of scholarship that critically examines issues related to the dynamic interplays between disability and various aspects of culture and society. Disability studies unites critical inquiry and political advocacy by utilizing scholarly approaches from the humanities, humanistic/post-humanistic social sciences, and the arts. When specifically applied to educational issues, it promotes the importance of infusing analyses and interpretations of disability throughout all forms of educational research, teacher education, and graduate studies in education. (DSE, ¶ 1).

Initial SIG efforts were aimed at disseminating information about disability studies, encouraging educational researchers to become interested in and use disability studies, and providing alternative ways to think and talk about disability in educational research.

Most of the authors in this book are active founding members of the AERA special interest group and have been instrumental in bringing together disability studies and educational research to the extent that it can now be considered to be a recognizable sub-field of study.

Since 1999, the field of disability studies in education in the US has grown to include: (1) numerous peer-reviewed publications; (2) a conference sponsored annually by National-Louis University in Chicago, led by Dr. Valerie Owen and the Louisiana Technological Institute/Louisiana Center for the Blind in Ruston, Louisiana, with the support of Dr. Ron Ferguson; and more recently, Teachers College in New York City, led by Dr. D. Kim Reid, David Connor, and Jan Valle; (3) a short-lived journal co-edited by Scot Danforth and Susan Gabel (*Disability, Culture and Education*); (4) annual SIG meetings and sessions at AERA; (5) this book series with Peter Lang (Disability Studies in Education) for which this is the first publication; 6) and, in addition to a long-standing program at Syracuse University, the emergence of numerous graduate concentrations and programs in disability studies/education (e.g., Teachers College, National College of Education at National-Louis University). Most recently, the Ontario Institute for Educational Studies announced its search for a faculty member in Disability Studies in Education. The rapid expansion of interest in disability studies in education in just five years demonstrates the relevance and importance of this field of inquiry for educational research and practice.

Social Interpretations of Disability

One hallmark of disability studies is its adherence to what has been called a "social model of disability" (Abberley, 1987), first suggested by Vic Finkelstein (1980) and other disability rights activists, in which disability is understood as a form of oppression. Although "social model" is the most common usage of the concept, I agree with Vic Finkelstein (2001, ¶ 2) that the phrase "social interpretation" is a better and more inclusive representation of disability studies standpoints. In this chapter, I use "social model" to refer to the traditional historical-materialist interpretation of disability. In contrast, I use "social interpretation" to refer to the wider array of disability theories in disability studies (e.g., disability identity, disability embodiment, disability discourse). As a whole, social interpretations of disability contrast with typical educational views wherein "disability" represents innate individual deficits. In disability studies, the disability-as-deficit notion is referred to as a clinical or medical model and is rejected as the basis for understanding the lived experiences of disabled people because it tends to pathologize difference and rely upon expert knowledge (i.e., physicians, special educators, rehabilitation counselors) to "remediate" difference (Society for Disability Studies, Guidelines for Disability Studies, ¶ 3).

It is fairly well accepted that the earliest formal expression of the social model originated in the disabled people's movement of the UK in 1975 when UPIAS issued a policy statement in which it argued that "the traditional way of dealing with disabled people has been for doctors and other professionals to decide what is best for us" (Section 14) and called for disabled people's resistance to the medicalization of disability and "the imposition of medical authority" (ibid.) over their lives. Shortly thereafter, in the *Fundamental Principles of Disability*, UPIAS framed the basic assumption of the social model.

> In our view, it is society which disabled physically impaired people. Disability is something that is imposed on top of our impairments by the way we are unnecessarily isolated and excluded from full participation in society. Disabled people are therefore an oppressed group in society. (3)

Not only did UPIAS stake out the origin of social interpretations of disability, it argued strongly against segregation and demanded the supports necessary to facilitate full inclusion in society, stating that those supports

> must include the necessary financial, medical, technical, educational and other help required from the State to enable us to gain maximum possible independence in daily living activities, to achieve mobility, to undertake productive work, and to live where and how we choose with full control over our lives. (¶ 1)

The American counterpart to the early social model, the minority group model, emerged in the late 1970s in the United States, and was clearly influenced by the American civil rights movement's claim about the social status of members of minority groups. Adherents claimed that minority group members experience marginalization, disenfranchisement, discrimination, stigmatization, and stereotyping as a result of their minority status (Schwartz, 1988, Rioux, 1991; Hahn, 1988; Wang, 1992; Pfeiffer, 1993). One early article by Robert Bogdan and Doug Biklen (1977) adapted the vocabulary of the civil rights movement, identifying "handicapism" (consistent with the popular use of "handicap" at that time) as "a set of assumptions and practices that promote the differential and unequal treatment of people because of apparent or assumed...differences" (15).

Ableism

Bogdan and Biklen's concept is still used today in the disability studies literature but in lieu of "handicapism," the term "ableism" is used. Various definitions of ableism exist. The *Hyperdictionary* defines ableism as "discrimination in favor of the able-bodied and able-minded." Some local school districts are giving attention to the term, as does the Peel District School Board of Mississauga, Ontario, Canada on its website's definition: "A set of practices and beliefs that assign inferior value (worth) to people who have developmental, emotional, physical, or psychiatric disabilities" (¶ 1). Thomas Hehir, former director of the US Department of Education's Office of Special Education Programs, former Associate Superintendent for the Chicago Public Schools, and former Director of Special Education in the Boston Public Schools, claims that ableism in education is, "The devaluation of disability" that "results in societal attitudes that uncritically assert that it is better for people to walk than roll, speak than sign, read print than read Braille, spell independently than use a spell-check, and hang out with nondisabled students as opposed to other disabled students" (Hehir, 2002, ¶ 7). These definitions and common usage indicate that ableism, entails: social biases against people whose bodies function differently than what is considered "normal," and beliefs and practices resulting from and interacting with the biases that serve to discriminate. The traditional social model would add that such practices do more than discriminate; they oppress.

Debates about Social Interpretations

In the late 1990s, the term "social model" became quite predominant among those in disability studies around the world, including scholars in the US, however such usages might be revised by Finkelstein's term, "social interpretation." Today, a myriad of interpretations and uses of the term "social model" can be found, including more traditional minority group model applications and as a result, when noting an author's claim to be using the "social model," it can be helpful to ask which version of the social model is being purported (Gabel and Peters, 2004). In fact, Gabel and Peters' review of the last decade of disability studies literature reveals that the social model is claimed by authors operating across paradigms, theoretical frameworks, and disciplinary boundaries. Given this, it might be of greatest usefulness to merely replace "social model" with "social interpretation(s)," as Finkelstein has suggested.

While both early social interpretations of disability (the traditional British version of the social model and the minority group model in the US) were concerned with the collective experience of a group of oppressed or marginalized people, subtle distinctions in discourse stemming from political and cultural differences distinguished them. Generally speaking, the UK version purported by UPIAS, and subsequently by sociologists in the UK, adhered to a sturdy neo-Marxist philosophy with clear delineations between disability (social oppression) and impairment (functional limitation) while the US version remained more eclectic, usually did not adamantly distinguish between disability and impairment and emphasized the social construction of disability rather than the sociopolitical processes of disablement.

In disability studies, as in identity politics in general, there have been tensions between competing political interests and agendas. This is particularly true in disability studies, however, because one defining characteristic of disability studies has been a rejection of the medical model, which is a highly individualized model of disability. Historically and for political purposes, the disability studies and disability rights communities have resisted individual interpretations of disability experiences and preferred interpretations of collective sociopolitical issues. It was argued that for too long, individualistic notions of disability focused on what was perceived as innate individual deficits (e.g., the medical model) and their amelioration at the expense of examining the social processes that disable individuals. Vic Finkelstein (2001), an important figure in the UK disability rights community and a member of the original team drafting the UPIAS *Fundamental Principles of Disability*, has gone so far as to argue that within the social interpretation of disability, "disabled people *are not* the subject matter" (1), suggesting that disablement (i.e., the social oppression of people with impairments) is the subject matter. However, when one examines the literature of the last eight or more years, this is not proven to be the case (Gabel and Peters, 2004). In fact, a good deal of social interpretation of disability examines lived experience and embodiment (e.g., Corker, 1999; Peters, 1996; Ghai, 2002, 2003; Thomas, 2001; Snyder and Mitchell, 2001). In *disability/postmodernism*, edited by Mairian Corker and Tom Shakespeare (2002), there is significant interest in embodiment. Authors explore, to name a few: touch, ethics, and disability (Price and Shildrick, 2002), desirability and the practice of the self in men with cerebral palsy (Shuttleworth, 2002), aesthetics of disability (Silvers, 2002), and madness and distress (Wilson and Beresford, 2002).

For a time, it seemed as though the importance of collective voice and political action outweighed concern for the individual, including the individual who resisted the dominant discourse of the disability rights movement. In 1996, Susan Peters argued against this radical stance, concluding that "individual perception is intertwined with collective identity, but must remain simultaneously independent of it...in order to change it" (231). Her suggestion, and the suggestion of other proponents of the identity model, was to "integrate the personal and political in an 'enduring hyphenation'" (ibid.). This concern for individual experience alongside collective experience is often discredited by those who find collective theories more compelling and politically efficacious.

In the late 1990s, some critics of these early strands of the social model argued that neither a pure Marxist structuralism, nor a less emphatic but still structural minority group model, nor the identity model—even with its nod to the individual—acknowledge and account for the subtleties and ambiguities inherent in the experiences of the disability community (and its individual members) that "privileges some impaired identities over others" (Humphrey, 2000, 63). In 1999 Mairian Corker, a Deaf scholar from the UK, suggested the following.

> Academics in the field of disability studies aim to develop a social theory of disability, which comes as close as possible to explaining the 'reality' of disabled people… However, pursuing this ideal may mean accepting that there will always be a gap between what any theory can offer, and what disabled people need to know in understanding and changing their lives—a gap that may be exacerbated by power and knowledge inequalities and by the research process (627-28).

Another social interpretation, and one that has been debated within the disability community and between disability sub-communities, has purported that disability is a phenomenon emerging and resulting from the values and practices embedded within culture and that there is, as a result, a disability culture (Peters, 2000). This literature points to a slowly growing body of comparative disability studies as evidence for the cultural construction of disability and the viability of disability culture (Peters, 2000). Susan Peters and Robert Chimedza have studied disability in the Zimbabwean context (2000). Susan Gabel (2001, 2004) has studied it in the context of South Asian Indian immigrants to the US. Other comparative studies exist in the broader field of disability studies but this is an untapped area of research in the disability studies in education community. Until we produce more comparative educational research, there is a wide body of comparative literature outside education.

Today's Eclecticism

Recently, disability studies has seen an emergence of voices arguing for eclecticism within the social model or the dissolution of the social model along with other meta-narratives. The influence of the humanities is evident here. Analysis of the programs of the annual meetings of SDS suggest that in the mid- to late 1990s the American field of disability studies was in transition toward a strong if not predominant influence from the humanities. In 1998 *The Chronicle of Higher Education*, Peter Monaghan noted that

> the new, humanities-oriented approach to disability studies borrows from…cultural studies, area studies, feminism, race-and-ethnic studies, and gay-and-lesbian studies. It is extensively informed by literary and cultural criticism, particularly of the post-structuralist variety, insofar as it pulls apart concepts about disability to see what cultural attitudes, antagonisms, and insecurities went into shaping them. (¶ 13)

For example, Tom Shakespeare and Nicholas Watson (2001) argue that the "strong social model," which they defended in an earlier article (1997) and which is the version mapped out by UPIAS and upheld by many who adhere to the traditional social model, is a "modernist theory of disability—seeking to provide an overarching meta-analysis covering all dimensions of every disabled person's experience" that "is not a useful or attainable concept" (19). Likewise, Gabel and Peters (2004), both disabled scholars, argue that we need to find "ways of theorizing disability more suited to current contexts and more responsive to emerging world trends" (586) and suggest that this might be done through the use of resistance theory to understand the complex relationships and negotiations between divergent ideas while also uniting the global disability community toward praxis.

Conceptual frameworks that encourage fluid ways of interpreting disability experiences and various critiques of the strong social model suggest that the social model, itself, may be replaced at some point in the future. The question is—with what? One suggestion comes from Gabel and Peters (2004) in an argument for using resistance theory to interpret disability to provide a way out of the determinist and universalist claims of the social model by offering a fluid, malleable theory "responsive to particular contexts" (593). They suggest that the social model, itself, emerged in resistance to the medical model and that resistance is inherent within all strands of the social model: resistance to stigma, disablement, social oppression, political and economic exclusion, etc. On the other hand, disabled people are not the only ones resisting. There is resistance *against* disabled people as well. A resistance theory of disability maintains the social model's focus on the politics of disablement and adds to it a recognition of the complexities of resistance as

> operating in all directions of the social sphere...Resistance functions as a way for disabled people to push against dominance while also attempting to pull society into disabled people's ways of seeing. (594-95)

This positions resistance as a multilevel, multidimensional dialectic within which there is push and pull, give and take, deconstruction/reconstruction between players at all levels of the social world. In addition to interpreting resistance as engagement in dichotomous processes, resistance theory also connotes an open-ended negotiation of meaning, a fluid dialectic movement without the constraints of time or space. It addresses the critics of the strong social model by opening up possibilities and blurring boundaries while it also avoids the theoretical tendency to construct abstract or rigid models from which action and social change cannot emerge.

The social model's rejection of the medical model continues to be a mainstay yet there is some internal resistance to outright rejection of the medical model. Gabel and Peters (2004) suggest that some benefits for disabled people have come from the scientific method underlying the medical model; for example, medications and other technologies that improve function. The danger, of course, is in the misapplication of the medical model to the social contexts of disability. Some of these misapplications include: using the medical model to diagnose, prescribe, and treat "conditions" that are the result of institutionalized oppression; adhering to the medical model's emphasis on individual pathology while ignoring social pathology; reproducing the myths used by the medical model (e.g., IQ) to stigmatize individuals and groups with labels; and dehumanizing individuals with functional limitations. There is also the danger—identified by various stakeholder groups—of the assimilation of disability culture through the use of the medical model to "cure" people when the results could be cultural genocide (e.g., curing deafness thereby eliminating Deaf culture, Tucker, 1998; or curing Dwarfism thereby eliminating Little People, Ricker, 1995).

Method in Disability Studies

Method in disability studies often follows the methodological traditions in the disciplines and has evolved over time, as have disciplinary traditions. One method in disability studies, sometimes referred to as the "emancipatory method" (Barnes, 2003; Duckett and Pratt, 2001; Walmsley, 2001; Davis, 2000; Kitchin, 2000), assumes that disabled people are the experts on disability and that their leadership and involvement in the research process is necessary for any research about them. Consider James Charlton's (1998) book title—*Nothing About Us Without Us*—as a mantra of the emancipatory research method. The basic assumption in the emancipatory method is that research must proceed with participation and leadership from disabled people to the greatest extent possible. Research agendas must be driven by the concerns defined by disabled people. It is assumed that when this is followed, disabled people's problems of access and liberation are more likely to be solved; emancipation is possible because disabled people are the ones who best know the issues and problems and can best frame the questions that guide research and the analysis of data gathered through research. The emancipatory research literature is very similar to what educators refer to as action research but tends to have a stronger emphasis on leadership and involvement by disabled people, or the group in whose interest the action research is being conducted. Ultimately, emancipatory research is concerned with a Freirian form of praxis, or a conscious effort at social change that brings about equity, social justice, and full participation in society where the work toward social change is led by those who are, themselves, oppressed.

One methodological dilemma for educators is the problem of deciding how to balance the need for the improvement of function (often the school's concern) with the refusal to pathologize and the reticence to "cure" difference (two concerns of social interpretations). In education, the balancing act becomes quite complex and the questions we ask as educators are often different than the questions asked by disability studies scholars and practitioners in other fields. For example: When does "difference" signal functional limitations to the extent that the individual needs intervention, support, or assistance different than is typically offered to students in order to benefit from education? This question does not assume that all forms of difference must be "cured." How and when do teachers and parents decide it is time for a special education referral? This question does not assume that a special education referral is the best option when students are struggling. How can students with significant educational needs get an appropriate education while simultaneously remaining full citizens of the school community? This question assumes that full citizenship mitigates against disablement. What is an appropriate education for students with significant educational needs? Are separate educational contexts ever warranted, and if so, under what conditions? These questions are skeptical of the assumption that students with significant educational needs require a separate education. Are separate contexts (i.e., self-contained classrooms) always oppressive or can they sometimes be liberatory, and who decides whether an educational context is oppressive or liberatory? This question assumes that there can be liberation and oppression in any educational context but interrogates the power relations in making claims about such matters. Is it possible to find the balance between individual educational preferences and school politics, and if so, what is that balance and how do we achieve it? This question assumes that tensions between individuals and institutions will exist even in the best of circumstances. What are the underlying assumptions in the "over-representation in special education" arguments; do those assumptions perpetuate disability stigma, and if so, how? This question assumes that ableism exists everywhere, even within standpoints that appear concerned with oppression and liberation. How can education be organized to prevent institutionalized oppression of any student? This question assumes that without educational praxis, disablement (or other forms of oppression) will occur. These questions are not asked often by scholars in disability studies but they are questions that disability studies in education must ask and answer.

Disability Studies in Education

In many ways, describing disability studies in education is like describing philosophy of education or history of education. One could define disability studies in education as the use and application of disability studies assumptions and methods to educational issues and problems. A later book in this series, *Vital Questions in Disability Studies in Education* (Danforth and Gabel, forthcoming), will map out the field in much greater depth and may contradict some of my points in this chapter. To begin thinking about disability studies in education, one can refer to the Society for Disability Studies (SDS, Guidelines for Disability Studies). While the guidelines are for programs in disability studies, they provide a sense of the landscape of disability studies from the perspective of the oldest scholarly society devoted to disability studies: 1) it is multi-/inter-disciplinary, 2) it "challenges the view of disability as an individual deficit that can be remediated" and explores the external factors (e.g., culture, society, economics, politics) that define people and "determine responses to difference," 3) it studies disability from national and international perspectives, 4) it encourages participation by disabled people and "ensures physical and intellectual access," and 5) it prioritizes leadership by disabled people while also welcoming the contributions of those who share the above goals. In the past, many scholars in disability studies have argued that disability studies is characterized by adherence to the "social model. " However, this is changing and as I have cited earlier in this chapter, many strong social modelists are recognizing the usefulness of perspectives in the humanities and post-structural social sciences.

On the other hand, there has been some conversation among Disability Studies in Education SIG Members (e.g., Ferri, 2003) about the potential contributions of educational research to disability studies. Perhaps this book can begin that conversation while also introducing graduate students and faculty in education to the field of Disability Studies in Education. The chapters herein provide examples of the ways in which the conversation can be mutually beneficial. Together, the chapters speak to most of the "Guidelines for Disability Studies" recommended by SDS and those not addressed have been discussed in some way in this chapter. Individually, these authors provide examples of the diversity of research interests, methods, and intersections between disability studies and educational research.

Negotiating Disability, Resisting Disablement

In chapters strongly influenced by disability studies in the humanities, Susan Gabel, Julie Allan, and Anne Ruggles Gere address the negotiation of meanings of disability with an emphasis on art and performativity. Each of them either explicitly or implicitly considers the ways in which the meaning of disability is negotiated through public sayings and doings of the body. In chapter 2, Gabel uses "an aesthetic of disability" to map out a process of "coming to know" disability through experience in the "web of relations." She describes the aesthetic as an "unbounded construct" that

> opens everything up to the possibilities of the disabled body, and the ways in which disability discourses of self and community create narratives of the art of experience. (22)

Gabel suggests that "the aesthetic allows movement all around and inside disability" while it subverts dominant aesthetics (or ways of coming to know something like disability), talks back to hegemony, and emerges from within experiences of disablement. She draws from feminist theory, aesthetic theory, disability theory, ethnographic research, politics, and art to construct an aesthetic of disability that offers options to the strong social model. She further claims that the aesthetic "creates spaces for interpretation that might not be available without the aesthetic framework." Gabel concludes with a discussion of how the aesthetic has useful applications in research, such as providing an alternative theoretical framework for inquiry and compelling particular interpretive devices.

Allan (chapter 3) argues that disability art is subversive and that disabled people "use their own bodies as weapons to subvert and undermine disabling barriers and name able-bodied people as part of the problem" (Allan, 37). Allan considers disability art as the performance of ideology and as a way to debate concepts and ideologies that guide policy and practice. Referencing works by Nancy Mairs, Cheryl Marie Wade, Audre Lorde, and Johnny Crescendo, Allan demonstrates the performativity of disability art; its ability to involve the audience and the artist in a shared ideological critique. Using the conceptual tool, kynicism, or lived pantomime, Allan reveals how the use of "subversive tactics"

> confront the pathetic phrases of the ruling ideology...mock solemnity through banality and ridicule, but [do] so by pragmatic, rather than argumentative, means. More precisely, its argument is pantomimic—lived rather than spoken—and inspired by cheekiness. (46)

Anne Ruggles Gere (chapter 4), on the other hand, takes a different and perhaps contrasting approach to performativity in her essay on in/visibility and the gaze. Using her daughter, an invisibly impaired woman (to use strong social model language), as her touchstone, Gere explores the spaces between visibility and invisibility. She complicates passing and surveillance. She interrogates the disability studies stance against passing, describing her daughter's struggles to understand herself as a disabled woman. "As Cindy's case illustrates," writes Gere,

> invisibility introduces the element of choice. Cindy, and those like her, can choose whether or not to reveal a condition. Invisibility enables them to avoid...the regulation that comes with visibility. As is true for any kind of passing, the choice of how to handle invisibility carries

risks, but the fact remains that disability is moved out of the realm of
the visible. (58)

In a sense, Gere is posing the problem of "reading another's body" (ibid.), of
being sure about what seems to be visible to us as we gaze upon the other.
For Gabel, getting past what is apparent to the meaning underneath would
represent an aesthetic process, a process of coming to know. Allan might add
that getting to the meaning underneath is aided by kynicism in disability art.
In contrast, Gere subtly challenges attempts to get at the invisible without
tallying the costs involved.

Reproducing Difference, Commodifying Disability

Historical-materialism, the philosophy of viewing the present in its
historical and physical world context, has a long tradition in disability
studies, particularly in the UK's strong social model. The next two chapters
take the historic-materialist stance; one, a macro-analysis, to argue against
the commodification of disability as a class category in education (Erevelles,
chapter 5); the other (Danforth, chapter 6) to reveal the danger of behavior
management as a means to commodify students labeled emotionally
behaviorally disordered (EBD).

In her chapter Nirmala Erevelles takes on critical pedagogy for its
inattention or "cursory gestures" (66) to disabled people. She frames a
materialist argument linking disability marginalization to other forms of
reproduced difference and class hierarchies in schools. Among those
students at the very bottom of the hierarchy, she argues, are students with
cognitive impairment; those students needing the most support to benefit
from their education. Disability is often used by critical theorists as a "true"
category, while other forms of difference (race, class, gender, etc.) are
considered re/produced forms, Erevelles argues. "The category of
disability," she claims, "is utilized by critical theorists as the boundary
condition that marks the limits of human agency" (70). Rather than
reconstituting their notion of human agency, they seem to have a-critically
applied it to people with significant cognitive needs. Viewing disabled
people as "critical agents" (71) is essential, according to Erevelles, as is
recognizing that they have been critical agents all along but have not been
viewed as such. Erevelles concludes with critique of the commodification of
disability—from which people with cognitive impairments have most
suffered—and a call for praxis.

Scot Danforth applies a similar theoretical framework to the micro-
level of the classroom to demonstrate the ways in which the use of token

economies separate students from meaningful learning opportunities and force them into "labor" that is "[d]enuded of moral or social value" (87). As a result of the use of tokens to reward compliant behavior, "the students' point-earning actions are alienated labor," claims Danforth, "that operate not to constitute and enhance the development of self in social context but to vacate and diminish the self as moral agent in the world" (ibid.). Rather than meeting the emotional needs of students, Danforth argues that these behavior management techniques produce students estranged from their work and from their teachers along five dimensions: powerlessness, meaninglessness, normlessness, isolation, and self-estrangement. Sadly, these dimensions represent the anti-thesis of the hope that special education has posited for the last fifty years.

Restorying Education, Supporting Praxis

The influence of humanities-based disability studies is reflected in Linda Ware's chapter (7), in which she links it with critical special education, which is the tradition of a small number of special educators who have challenged the "well-entrenched culture of traditional special education" that emerged from within the medical model. Ware suggests a "restorying" of special education and uses her work with school teachers as an example of the possibilities. Through in-depth engagement with disability studies texts, members of the disability community, and curriculum, Ware describes teachers' responses to the insights offered by humanities-based disability studies. "Teachers expressed awe," she writes, "at the multiple interpretations given to disability and its place in our lives as reflected in the lectures and materials we reviewed" (112). Ware continues:

> Approaching disability from a humanities perspective suggests to some the potential for society to more fully understand disability, and therefore, to teach more rich and varied accounts of living with disability. The project seemed timely as K-12 classrooms, like society has become more heterogeneous than at any time in the past. (ibid.)

Ware's call for schools to "accept the challenge that disability studies present and begin to include disability lessons informed by "pride and empowerment" challenges disability studies in education to create ways for schools to go beyond accepting the challenge toward actually educating for pride and empowerment.

Ware's claims about curriculum possibilities contrast starkly Ellen Brantlinger's chapter (8) in which she deconstructs two shibboleths in education; two basic assumptions that have constrained curriculum possibilities. Brantlinger is a critical special educator who paved the way for many of who have walked in her footsteps. In her chapter, she provides evidence of deficit thinking at work at the broad systemic and curricular levels through her analysis of developmentally appropriate practice and individualized instruction. She argues that these two basic assumptions have significant effects on programming and curriculum, and ultimately, practice in early childhood education and special education. Brantlinger finds that their use creates inequities for disabled students: special education curriculum becomes watered down in the attempt to provide "individualized instruction" for students based on their labels and perceived performance, and they are not given age-appropriate opportunities in the attempt to follow developmentally appropriate practices in which students must meet one developmental milestone before proceeding to the next. Such instructional decisions, Brantlinger argues, produces and contributes to the achievement gap, particularly for minority children. Furthermore, they do not make good use of what is known about the learning process as dynamic and fluid. Nor do they acknowledge the normalcy of difference in the classroom and the importance of classroom communities that embrace differences.

Deborah Gallagher (chapter 9), another critical special educator, is also critical of educators who adhere to traditions that exacerbate social conditions. In her chapter, Gallagher critiques objectivist technical rationality, implicitly recalling Brantlinger's critique of developmentally appropriate practice. Both authors confront fundamental assumptions in special and general education when considering pedagogy for disabled students. Gallagher notes that technical rationality has created

> an increasing emphasis on measurable "basic skills" instruction, lockstep curricula with accompanying basal textbook adoption, and pedagogical procedures that have gone from the merely prescriptive to the literally scripted. (139)

Gallagher further argues that such emphases are often the hallmark of special education pedagogy, as though "they need more of what is good for all students" (139-40), and as if increased rehearsal of repetitious, rote content is, in fact, good for any student. One might also note that such approaches sound all too familiar due to recent No Child Left Behind legislation and the trend toward high stakes testing that pressures teachers into standardized curriculum and direct instruction rather than constructivist pedagogy. Gallagher provides the historical context for the technical rationalist standpoint, links this to the deskilling of teachers and the disabling of students, and proposes a constructivist and inclusive approach to education that encourages teachers to stop looking "outside themselves" for what defines their work (e.g., teacher's manuals, standardized tests, and the perfect strategy). Rather, Gallagher argues that the answer is not outside the teacher, implying that it is inward; in one's intuition, values, oneself, and in knowing one's students.

One of the criticisms of current disability studies approaches is that they tend to be too focused on theory and too unconcerned with practice. As with other new theoretical standpoints (e.g., feminist theory, race theory, gender theory), and in our efforts to advance social interpretations of disability, it is the case that we have ignored the very real needs of practitioners for conversations between theory and practice and concrete examples of social interpretations in practice. It is clear that there is a need to figure out how to talk about disability studies in ways that make sense for educational policy and practice and that we need to observe and learn from teachers who are practicing liberatory pedagogy and who can work together to translate social interpretations into practice. It is anticipated that later books in this series will address real issues of practice. This will be difficult because most educational policy and practice is built upon the medical model of disability. However, it can help if we recognize current research and practice that is consistent with a disability studies perspective and build upon that.

Susan Peters' chapter (10) provides an example of the kind of pedagogical possibilities we can offer to teachers. She describes her use of Freirian critical pedagogy in her literacy work with urban high school students labeled learning disabled. She compares this work to efforts of the Zimbabwean Disability Rights Movement (DRM), noting the similarities in process (meeting together in small groups over an extended period of time), goals (conscientization, or a collective sense of the injustices they were experiencing), and outcomes (praxis, or taking action against those injustices to create a better world). While the Zimbabwean context differs dramatically from the urban African American one Susan describes, the two (a national civil rights movement and a high school literacy movement) share important similarities, which Peters describes. In Zimbabwe, the movement resisted oppressive sociopolitical conditions while in the American high school, students resisted coerced identities and struggled to reconstruct chosen identities.

Conclusion

To return to the simple description of disability studies in education, disability studies in education is concerned with issues and problems of education, broadly construed, that affect or are affected by disablement in educational contexts. Disability studies in education is primarily concerned with the view of issues and problems as defined by disabled people and as they relate to social exclusion and oppression. These are broad categories, however, and can include economic, political, historical, and other institutions when examined through the social lens. Since it is concerned with the full range of educational issues, disability studies in education is not limited solely to issues and problems in special education. At first, this can seem counterintuitive to educators who have spent their careers putting disability into a special education box. However, disabled students and teachers can be found throughout public and private schools, traditional and nontraditional educational settings, and pre-kindergarten through higher education. Furthermore, educational disablement often begins in general education settings, as when reasonable accommodations are refused, school communities are exclusive, parents believe their child with an impairment will not receive equitable treatment in general education, or the necessary resources for full inclusion are not provided. In fact, there are those using disability studies whose research remains grounded outside special education or disability studies, such as those in curriculum studies (Baker, 2002a, 2002b), educational foundations (Erevelles, 2000), and history of education (Seldon, 1999, 2000; Goodman, 2003). I propose that the wider we cast the net, the more influence disability studies in education will have, and the more we influence education research, theory, and practice, the more likely we can successfully work toward social justice in all educational contexts.

References

Abberley, P. (1987). The concept of oppression and the development of a social theory of disability. *Disability and Society* 2(1), 5–20.from http://www.medanthronet/ research/disability/index.html.

Baker, B. (2002a). The hunt for disability: The new eugenics and the normalization of school children. *Teachers College Record* 104, 663–703.

———— (2002b). Disorganizing educational tropes: Conceptions of dis/ability and curriculum. *Journal of Curriculum Theorizing 18(4)*, 47–80.

Barnes, C. (2003). What a difference a decade makes: Reflections on doing 'emancipatory' disability research. *Disability and Society 18(1)*, 3–17.

Bogdan, R., & Biklen, D. (1977). Handicapism. *Social Policy* March/April, 14–19.

Charlton, J. (1998). *Nothing about us without us: Disability oppression and empowerment*. Berkeley: University of California Press.

Corker, M., & Shakespeare, T. (Eds.). (2002). d*isability/postmodernity: embodying disability theory*. London/New York: Continuum.

Corker, M. (1999). Differences, conflations, and foundations: The limits to 'accurate' theoretical representation of disabled people's experience? *Disability and Society 14(5)*, 627–42.

Danforth, S., & Gabel, S. (forthcoming). *Vital Questions for Disability Studies in Education*. New York: Peter Lang Publishers.

Davis, J. (2000). Disability studies as ethnographic research and text: Research strategies and role for promoting social change? *Disability and Society 15(2)*, 191–206.

Disability Studies in Education. *About DSE: Objectives*. Retrieved July 10, 2004, from http://ced.ncsu.edu/2/dse/.

Duckett, P. S., & Pratt, R. (2001). The researched opinions on research: Visually impaired people and visual impairment research. *Disability and Society 16(6)*, 815–35.

Erevelles, N. (2000). Educating unruly bodies: Critical pedagogy, disability, and the politics of schools. *Educational Theory 50(1)*, 25–48.

Ferri, Beth. (2003). Personal conversation.

Finkelstein, V. (1980). Attitudes and disabled people: Issues for discussion. Retrieved September 30, 2004 from http://www.leeds.ac.uk/disability-studies/archiveuk/finkelstein/attitudes.pdf.

———— (2001). *The Social Model of Disability Repossessed*. Retrieved September 15, 2004, from http://www.leeds.ac.uk/disabilitystudies/archiveuk/finkelstein/soc%20mod%20repossessed.pdf.

Gabel, S. (2004). South Asian Indian Cultural Orientations Toward Mental Retardation. *Mental Retardation 42(1)*, 12–25.

Gabel, S., Vyas, S., Patel, H., Patel, S. (2001). Problems of methodology in cross-cultural disability studies: An indian immigrant example. In Barnartt, S., & Altman, B. (Eds.), *Exploring theories and expanding methodologies: Where we are and where we need to go*, 209-28. Oxford, UK: Elsevier Science Ltd.

Gabel, S., & Peters, S. (2004). Presage of a paradigm shift? Beyond the social model of disability toward a resistance theory of disability. *Disability and Society 19(6)*, 571–596.

Ghai, A. (2003). *(Dis)Embodied forms: Issues of disabled women*. New Delhi, India: Shakti Books.

———— (2002). Disability in the Indian context: Post-colonial perspectives. In M. Corker and T. Shakespeare (Eds.), *Disability/postmodernity: Embodying disability theory*, 88–100. London/New York: Continuum.

Goodman, J. (2003). Reflections on researching an archive of disability: Sandlebridge, 1902-1935. *Educational Review 35(1)*, 47–54.

Hahn, H. (1988). The politics of physical differences: Disability and discrimination. *Journal of Social Issues 44*, 47–49.

Hehir, Thomas. (2002). Eliminating ableism in education [Electronic version]. *Harvard Educational Review* 72. Retrieved September 30, 2004, from http://gseweb. harvard.edu/~hepg/hehir.htm.

Humphrey, J. (2000). Researching disability politics, or, some problems with the social model in practice. *Disability and Society 15(1)*, 63-86.

Hyperdictionary. Ableism. Retrieved August 10, 2004, from http://www. hyperdictionary.com/dictionary/ableism.

Kitchin, R. (2000). The researched opinions on research: Disabled people and disability research. *Disability and Society 15(1)*, 25–47.

Modern Language Association. Committee on Issues in the Profession. Retrieved July 5, 2004 from http://www.mla.org/comm_disability.

Monaghan, P. (1998). Pioneering field of disability studies challenges established approaches and attitudes [Electronic version]. *Chronicle of Higher Education.* Retrieved May 25, 2004, from http://www.uic.edu/orgs/sds/articles.html.

Peel District School Board. (Fall 2002). *Ableism Issue Paper #2 (Full Discussion).* Retrieved September 20, 2004, from http://www.gobeyondwords. org/documents/AbleismFullDiscussion.doc.

Peters, S. (2000). Is there a disability culture? A syncretisation of three possible world views. *Disability and Society 15(4)*, 583–601.

———— (1996). The politics of disability identity. In L. Barton (Ed.), *Disability and society: Emerging issues and insights*, 215–234. New York: Pergamon.

Peters, S., & Chimedza, R. (2000). Conscientization and the cultural politics of education: A radical minority perspective. *Comparative Education Review 44(3)*, 245–271.

Pfeiffer, D. (1993). The problem of disability definition, again. *Disability and Rehabilitation 21*, 392–96.

Price, J., & Shildrick, M. (2002). Bodies together: touch, ethics and disability. In M. Corker and T. Shakespeare (Eds.), *Disability/postmodernity: Embodying disability theory*, 62–75. London/New York: Continuum.

Ricker, R. (1995). *Do we really want this? Little people of America inc. comes to terms with genetic testing.* Retrieved August 10, 2004, from http://home.earthlink.net/ ~dkennedy56/dwarfism_genetics.html.

Rioux, M. (1991). Rights, justice, power: An agenda for change, a culture of diversity, rights-based technology. *Abilities Magazine* Autumn, 58-59.

Schwartz, H. (1988). Further thoughts on a "sociology of acceptance" for disabled people. *Journal of Social Policy* Fall, 36–39.

Selden, S. (2000). Eugenics and the construction of merit, race and disability. *Journal of Curriculum Studies 32(2)*, 235–252.

———— (1999). Inheriting shame: The story of eugenics and racism in america. New York: Teachers College Press.

Shakespeare, T., Watson, N. (2001). The social model of disability: An outdated ideology? In Barnartt, S., & Altman, B. (Eds.), *Exploring theories and expanding methodologies: Where we are and where we need to go*, 9–28. Oxford, UK: Elsevier Science Ltd.

———— (1997). Defending the social model. *Disability and Society 12(2)*, 293–300.

Shuttleworth, R. (2002). Defusing the adverse context of disability and desirability as a practice of the self for men with cerebral palsy. In M. Corker and T.

Shakespeare (Eds.), *Disability/postmodernity: Embodying disability theory*, 112–126. London/New York: Continuum.

Silvers, A. (2002). The crooked timber of humanity: Disability, ideology and the aesthetic. In M. Corker and T. Shakespeare (Eds.), *Disability/postmodernity: Embodying disability theory*, 228–244. London/New York: Continuum.

Snyder, S., & Mitchell, D. (2001). Re-engaging the body: Disability studies and the resistance to embodiment. *Public Culture 13*, 367–389.

Society for Disability Studies. *Mission Statement*. Retrieved July 5, 2004, from http://www.uic.edu/orgs/sds/generalinfo.html.

Thomas, C. (2001). Feminism and disability: The theoretical and political significance of the personal and the experiential. In L. Barton (Ed.), *Disability, politics and the struggle for change*, 48–58. London: David Fulton Publishers, Ltd.

Tucker, B. P. (1998). *Deaf culture, cochlear implants, and elective disability*. Retrieved August 10, 2004, from http://www.ncbi.nlm.nih.gov/entrez/query.fcgi?cmd=Retrieve&db=PubMed&list_uids=9762533&dopt=Abstract.

Union of the Physically Impaired Against Segregation. (1975). *Fundamental principles of disability*. Retrieved July 5, 2004, from http://www.leeds.ac.uk/disability-studies/archiveuk/UPIAS/fundamental%20principles.pdf.

Walmsley, J. (2001). Normalisation, emancipatory research and inclusive research in learning disability. *Disability and Society 16(2)*, 187–205.

Wang, C. (1992). Culture, meaning and disability: Injury prevention campaigns and the production of stigma. *Science and Medicine 35*, 1093–1102.

Wilson, A., & Beresford, P. (2002). Madness, distress and postmodernity: putting the record straight. In M. Corker and T. Shakespeare (Eds.), *Disability/postmodernity: Embodying disability theory*, 143–158. London/New York:Continuum.

2 An Aesthetic of Disability

Susan Gabel

> Understanding the capacity of aesthetic discourse can lead us to an aesthetic that makes disability powerful.
>
> (Silvers, 2002, p. 230)

Though still a matter of contestation today, the mid- to late 1990s was a time of even greater debate about what constitutes disability. In disability studies in the United States, the late 1990s were years of particular tension between the foundational disciplines of disability studies (the social sciences) and scholarship emerging from within the humanities. In 1996-1997, when I was writing my dissertation and was immersed in these debates, I was struggling to find a way to understand disability that accounted for both individual and collective experience, that avoided the hard-line structuralist standpoint of medical and educational models of disability, as well as the materialist stance found in the UK version of the "strong social model" (Shakespeare and Watson, 2001) of disability at the time. I also intuited that there must be more to disability than what was explained by the minority group model or identity version of disability theory prevalent in the US disability studies movement at the time. I was searching for something that opened up opportunities for playful and embodied narratives of disability. In the dissertation, I used three conceptual tools to weave together an aesthetic of disability: the body, disability, and experience. I argued that the aesthetic theory of John Dewey (1926, 1934) could be applied to disability as a lived experience to understand the ways in which disabled individuals interact with the social world to construct the disability identity. My approach accounted for the influence of social institutions on the emergence of the self but because it was grounded in Deweyan aesthetics and the self, it relied too heavily on the individual as an autonomous agent.

Since 1997, I have utilized an aesthetic orientation toward disability in most of my research and continue to elaborate on how it can be applied to a social model of disability in ways that make the social model more flexible, fluid, and permeable. In this chapter, however, I approach the aesthetic from a different angle and with a slightly different intent than I have in the past. Rather than considering ways in which disability can be understood through the lens of Deweyan aesthetics, I propose that disability can be understood *as an aesthetic*. By this I mean that my previous uses of the aesthetic were an attempt to understand disability (whatever it might be) by using aesthetics; but now, I am attempting to understand disability, itself, as an aesthetic process.

I see the aesthetic as a way of creating a postmodern discourse of disability with more subtlety and ambiguity than inheres within the predominant versions of the social model. This is possible in part because aesthetic discourse offers the flexibility that other more rigid discourses cannot provide. When used generally and as an unbounded construct, the aesthetic allows for thinking about disability as more than membership in a minority group or as a sign of oppression. It opens everything up to the possibilities of the disabled body, and the ways in which disability discourses of self and community create narratives of the art of experience. The aesthetic allows movement all around and inside disability. In the most general sense, I see aesthetization as one way of coming to know something.

I begin this chapter with John Dewey's general theory of aesthetics and offer embellishments from feminist, neo-Marxist, and disablist versions of the aesthetic. This frames disability as, admittedly, a poststructural and postmodern aesthetic; almost but not quite an anti-aesthetic (Armstrong 2000). In the second section, I directly address an aesthetic of disability and give examples of it. I conclude with suggestions for the application of an aesthetic of disability in educational research.

The Aesthetic

Art traditionally has been considered to be a perceptual object intentionally produced to elicit a certain kind of aesthetic experience (Beardsley, 1958/81). This aesthetic can be objectively defined, "...named and talked about [and] that characteristics can be attributed to" (17). The concerns of this brand of aesthetics are related to what is "true" about "art," and "what reason there is to believe that it is true" (8). Aesthetic value must be attributable to an object in order for it to be considered art and that value must be represented in objective terms. Perhaps the most prominent value is of "beauty." For the traditionalist, saying that a work of art is "beautiful" is essentially saying that regardless of how the work is related to anything else in the world, it has some kind of inherent worth that can be described a "beauty."

Dewey's Aesthetic

For John Dewey (1926, 1934), however, art is intimately and subjectively connected to everyday human experience, perhaps even synonymous with experience (Armstrong, 2000). It is crafted from the messiness of life. Isobel Armstrong writes that in Dewey's aesthetic, "the artwork does not *lead* to experience but *'constitutes one'*...because experience is interactive, the sum of interactivity which is always double at the same time as it dissolves dualism" (164). Art is the result of the attempt to express meaning through everyday activity and the give and take of social life; and rather than a prescribed value with objective parameters, the aesthetic is the meaning constructed from artful experience by those having an experience.

Philip Jackson (2002) demonstrates the thick layers and rich interpretations possible in aesthetic discourse. He references a 1906 speech to art teachers in which Dewey said that

> To feel the meaning of what one is doing, and to rejoice in that meaning; to unite in one concurrent fact the unfolding of the inner life and the ordered development of material conditions—that is art. (Quoted in Jackson, 2002, 292)

Notice the emphasis on *feeling* meaning. Jackson notes that Dewey's emphasis refers to the meanings that are wholly convincing—as if "felt in one's bones." They are an active work in progress, or as Dewey writes, "ends-in-view...things viewed after deliberation as worthy of attainment and as evocative of effort" (1926, 104). In Dewey's aesthetics, the production of art is what today might be referred to as an embodied act.

Dewey's concise definition of art includes his belief that art can produce moments of joy. The potential for pleasure, indicates Jackson, is the "promise of art" in Dewey's theory. However, if one were to read Dewey further, one would miss an important aspect of Dewey's aesthetic because for Dewey, art is grounded in the everyday world of human experience, and he freely admits that human experience involves struggle and tension; or, as Dewey puts it, "the doings and sufferings that form experience...a union of the precarious and the novel, irregular with the settled, assured and uniform..." (1926, 358). Here, Dewey not only recognizes suffering as part of the human condition; he also acknowledges the struggle we face to balance these tensions inherent to lived experience.

Art and the aesthetic are grounded in both the material world (which for Dewey includes language and meaning and, by extension, the social world) and the "inner life" of the self. Art is an expression of meaning that must be *read* and we learn to *read* art "with time and guided practice," suggests Jackson, through which "we become increasingly proficient in figuratively *seeing* what [is] mean[t]" (2002, 174). Dewey himself argues that aesthetic meanings come to us "clothes [and] originated in custom and tradition" (1926, 26). In other words, Dewey recognizes the historicity of the aesthetic but while the cloak of history surrounds art and the aesthetic, until meaning is assigned to art, there is no aesthetic.

Jackson continues with an explanation of Dewey's concern for the expressive meaning of art by noting "if there is a single message that reverberates throughout his writings on aesthetics it is that through a tendency to neglect the expressive dimensions of meaning, we live impoverished lives both individually and collectively" (173). But "expressive meaning tends to be opaque," lying "beneath the surface," and "waiting to be *read* by someone skilled in such reading" (ibid.). It is this reading applied to a work of art (or experience) that becomes the aesthetic. The kind of reading to which Dewey and Jackson are referring is not what one does when leafing through a magazine while waiting for a turn at the checkout counter. This reading entails a thoroughly involved subject

> engrossed with what one is doing...feel[ing] deeply about its meaningfulness...undergo[ing], even if only for a time, the near-erasure of the traditional distinction between inner and outer, subjective and objective... feel[ing] as one with the object taking form under one's own agency—that...is what it means to be artfully engaged in doing something. (Jackson, 2002, 174)

Dewey's concept of art and the aesthetic is central to what it means to be a whole human being. "It is to erase the distinction between thinking and feeling. It is to restore unity to the separation of subject and object. It is to live holistically, at least for a time" (176).

For Dewey, then, art is the result of fully engaged human experience in the everyday world. It could be found hung on a wall in a museum but it could also be found in the discourse of life, and this is where Dewey comes close to a postmodernist aesthetic. He very nearly acknowledges that art resides in the actual experience itself and that experience is given meaning through language ("the tool of tools")—an aesthetic discourse applied to lived experience. A slight postmodern twist while reading Dewey allows the leap I make here: if art is grounded in everyday human experience (the "doings and sufferings" that are "felt in one's bones"), and if language is used to create meaning from experience (aesthetic discourse), then art *is* experience (at least in some way) and the meaning created from experience is the aesthetic. I return to this argument later when I explore an aesthetic of disability.

A Solidarity Aesthetic

While Dewey's aesthetic acknowledges the importance of history for aesthetic meaning, as an aesthetic centering on the individual it misses an opportunity to connect individual and collective experience and to explore ways in which the two are mutually informative. Since collective experience plays a key role in feminist aesthetics, I next turn to some examples from feminist theory. Peggy Zeglin Brand (1995), a feminist philosopher, claims that art must be evaluated and aesthetic notions must develop from the context in which the art is produced. This results in a diverse aesthetic rather than a reproduction of the dominant aesthetic. In Brand's view, aesthetic values are the result of the political and ideological tradition in which one is immersed and are related to other values, such as values about justice, oppression, freedom, or diversity (268). Rather than an objectively derived value, such as the value Sotheby's might assign to a painting by Warhol or Rembrandt, Brand's use of the aesthetic is grounded in embodied life and culture and it is from within collective experience that aesthetic notions develop. She claims that

> We must become accustomed to relying upon more than one single monolithic sense of "aesthetic" as established by tradition. If a feminist sense of aesthetic value emerges as well as a black sense as well as a Native American sense, then so be it. (268)

Her subject, or the one creating aesthetic meaning, speaks with the authority of those who experience the very thing being appreciated and do so from within a community of shared experience. Here, authority is used to refer to epistemic privilege, or the notion that the one having an experience is best suited to give meaning to the experience (Alcoff and Potter, 1992; Bar on, 1992). Brand's is a solidarity aesthetic, in a sense, in which a community "agrees," in general, on an aesthetic. This agreement might be seen in what constitutes humor, preferences for and responses to literature or film, or ideas about which bodies are considered beautiful. Outsiders, or non-members, often find the aesthetic sense of others confusing, offensive, or meaningless. For example, as with most communities, the disability community has its own sense of humor and preferences in stories, art, music, and other forms of expression. Riva Lehrer, a disabled artist, represents the disability community's sense of the aesthetic when she paints the portraits of disabled people who have been important in her life. In the documentary about her art (Snyder and Mitchell, 2004), her subjects talk about their pleasure at seeing disabled people who use wheelchairs and have lumpy bodies or missing body parts portrayed as beautiful, powerful, mythical, mysterious and as boldly "staring back" at the viewer. As a woman with depression and the mother of a daughter with schizophrenia and cerebral palsy, I particularly enjoy tales of "surviving" the psychiatric system and watching my daughter dance in her wheelchair, legs flopping off her footrests, a grin on her face, arms moving slightly off beat with her own rhythmic syncopation.

These examples relate to Dewey's claim that art is bound to the "doings and sufferings that form experience" that he describes as "precarious," "novel," and "irregular." In his work, Dewey is careful to show that the aesthetic, which in this sense is a collective standpoint aesthetic, is interwoven with the joy and struggle of human existence as it erupts from within culture and history. This is reminiscent of the segment in the documentary "When Billy Broke His Head...and Other Tales of Wonder" (Simpson and Golfus, 1994), when Neil Marcus, a standup comedian and actor who has cerebral palsy, is performing a routine in which he is trying to order a hamburger over the phone. He says, "I want to order a hamburger," but he is difficult to understand. The actor on the other phone says, "You want what?" Marcus again says, "I want to order a hamburger." Again, the other actor does not understand what is being said. Marcus repeats, "I want to order a hamburger." The listener replies, "You want to order a hamburger?" Marcus jumps and yells, "Yes!" and the person on the other end explains, "He wants to order a hamburger!" Not only is this comedy routine generated from the "doings and sufferings that form experience," but it is precarious (e.g., Marcuse engages in a risky speech act) and irregular (literally, in his speech and figuratively, in the communicative act). This sketch speaks directly to the solidarity of experience disabled people share as they take risks interacting with the world.

A Transgressive Aesthetic

Bat Ami Bar on (1992) describes a related feminist standpoint aesthetic in which perspective results from the position one holds in a social system wherein one's relative distance to or from the center or the dominant aesthetic is key. Transgression is integral to this marginal aesthetic because it serves as a "function of the distance from the center...the more distant one is from the center, the more advantageous is one's points of view" (89). A transgressive aesthetic makes the privilege of the dominant aesthetic visible by revealing experience from outside hegemony. This argument contends that when we view the world from the position of privilege, it is difficult to see our privilege and, perhaps worse, it is difficult to see how we marginalize those who are not privileged with us. Bar on sees the marginal aesthetic as dangerous because it resides in what bel hooks (1990) describes as "a space of radical openness" (150), a place where anything is possible and the possibilities are subversive.

While Dewey's aesthetist could be (but is not necessarily) an art lover or a literature buff thoroughly immersed in a painting but not having experienced what is happening in the painting and not having painted it, the solidarity or standpoint aesthetic described by Brand and the marginal aesthetic of Bar on are immersed in the creating of art *and* its aesthetic through having embodied the art and the aesthetic. Diego Rivera's murals, Solzhenitsyn's *Gulag Archipelago*, Billy Golfus's documentary, and Neil Marcus's comedy act are examples of living within art and the aesthetic. Bar on privileges the marginal aesthetic above others and suggests that we "understand marginalization as a position and place of resistance" (1992, 87) against oppression.

A De/ReConstructive Aesthetic

Similarly, Herbert Marcuse (1978) views art and the aesthetic as *intrinsically* subversive. Art *is* resistance, and is essential for any revolution, he argues, because

> as ideology, it opposes the given society. The autonomy of art contains the categorical imperative: "things must change." If the liberation of human beings and nature is to be possible at all, then the social nexus of destruction and submission must be broken. (9)

Art is at once destructive and reconstructive. "The truth of art," Marcuse writes, "lies in its power to break the monopoly of established reality (i.e., of those who established it) to *define* what is *real*" (9). In Marcusean terms, the world of art is "more real than reality itself" (22) and operates out of a "desperate struggle for changing the world" (69). Through the subversive act of creating art, the artist produces aesthetic experiences that open up the possibilities for new social, political, and economic realities. For Marcuse, the artist points the way, creates the vision, builds a new world order, and does so with the tools of resistance and deconstruction.

In relation to art-as-resistance, there are numerous examples of artistic resistance to racial and ethnic dominance. First, consider the ethnic and sub-culture art that forms resistance of dominant US culture by revealing alternative possibilities and realities: gang graffiti, the Latino murals of Los Angeles and San Diego, or the slave myths and folktales in which stories of liberation and freedom are embedded.

The uses of art have not gone unnoticed by disability studies scholars. In contrast with the above examples, wherein art is used to represent counter-hegemony, many in disability studies have argued that art has reproduced hegemony by vilifying disabled people through representing them as deviant, hideous, and frightening. The Hunchback of Notre Dame is an often-cited reference. David Mitchell and Sharon Snyder (1997) argue that the Hunchback is an example of the "representational double bind of disability" (6) in which disabled people are marginal, liminal, and invisible while simultaneously they are used as the "raw materials out of which other socially disempowered communities make themselves visible" (ibid.). By this, Mitchell and Snyder mean that disability is used as a symbol for the deficits hegemonically assumed to inhere within those who are members of other marginal group categories (e.g., race, gender, class, sexual orientation). They complain that the body—as raced, classed, gendered, sexualized—is a popular site of analysis while at the same time most scholars ignore *disability;* rather, they use disability as a way of revealing racial and other stereotypes. Frankenstein's monster is an example of a body "pieced together out of the fabric of race, class, gender, and sexuality" (7), they argue; the result of which is a perfect metaphor for disability: a mute or speech-impaired, behaviorally disordered beast, dangerous to himself and others. (This is a representation that, in special education, would be referred to as "multiple handicaps," and which could result in attempts to assure "the safety of everyone" with a segregated program.)

Contrary to Mitchell and Snyder's arguments about art and the representation of disability, Anita Silvers (2002) describes an aesthetic in which disability is integrally woven into the themes and patterns of art; and rather than providing the typical postmodern account of representing disability as "fortifying the exclusionary applications of political power to which real disabled people are subjected" (230), Silvers describes representations of disability as reflective of artistic acknowledgment of human frailty. She writes:

> Disabled people sometimes protest that art rarely reflects the lumpy, bumpy, dumpy realities of their lives. But relatively few artistic works about any subject are so very realistic. Versions of the thesis that artistic representations of disability lack the disagreeable aspects of real life with a disability all fail because it is hard to see what kind of

disagreeableness can inhere in real disabled people but cannot do so in artistic imitations of them. Moreover, from a postmodern perspective, fidelity to the real is no criterion by which to judge art. (231)

Silvers argues that disability gets no special treatment in art and, in fact, is often used as a counter-hegemonic device. She continues by claiming that art has a history of appreciation and celebration of difference on one hand and the function of exposure of hegemony on the other hand. Consider, for example, the Venus de Milo's missing limbs. Silvers argues that the novelty of the disabled body, rather than beauty in a hegemonic sense, is a thing of power. Beauty is common and respectable, suggests Silvers, but

> the privilege of being disabled is acknowledgement of a claim to having one's *difference* respected (emphasis added). Though about this way, normalcy and disability not only are concordant (rather than oppositional) but are vitally so. (238)

The result is that "aesthetizing disability elevates otherness to originality" (241) and this, she argues, is the power of aesthetic discourse.

While I agree with Silvers that aesthetic discourse can "make disability powerful," I believe she stops too short in her discussion of the aesthetic and in doing so, she does not take full advantage of the power of the aesthetic as a tool for social change. A less constricted notion of "aesthetic" would avoid gluing the aesthetic onto an object (e.g., a statue, a painting, a text, an observable "work" of art). Rather, an understanding of the aesthetic as a fluid, ephemeral process of coming to understand and appreciate something would make an aesthetic of disability a sociopolitical tool on a larger scale—something "dangerous" by ableist standards.

An example of the large-scale "danger" of an aesthetic of disability is found in the late 1990s struggle by disability activists to have the Roosevelt memorial in Washington, DC, depict Roosevelt sitting in his wheelchair. At the time, the need for this struggle was interpreted by many in disability studies as an example of the ableist view that people do not want to admit a US President could have been "weak" or "impaired" or "sick." If one accepts the traditional disability studies argument that disability has historically been used to represent such characteristics, it makes sense to interpret the struggle over the memorial this way. On the other hand, consider the possibility that depicting a President as disabled is such a revolutionary, transgressive, resistant act that ableists, including many disabled people, could not bring themselves to consider it. For people who view the world this way, confronting the image of a powerful man sitting in a wheelchair could be too risky. Here is possible evidence of the transformative power and danger of an aesthetic of disability: resistance to the location of disability in power.

The question is, does disability weaken the powerful and our image of them or do such representations strengthen disability and the disabled? Does recognition of human frailty in the powerful make others less inclined to follow them or more inclined to be skeptical of them? Does resistance to locating disability in power come from the belief that disability cannot be powerful or from the collective shame about disabling people because of their difference? Is it more possible to marginalize disabled people when power is disassociated from disability? I argue that it is more likely that all of these possibilities are simultaneously at play, that the resulting social relations cause confusion and make the world seem unstable, and that attempts to make disability invisible are not only attempts to sustain the image of power and maintain power relations but that they are also attempts to prevent the unleashing of the power of an aesthetic of disability.

An Aesthetic of Disability

Now stepping back to fit the previous themes into an aesthetic of disability, I draw from Dewey but give his version a postmodern twist. If experience is art and the body is lived experiences, then the aesthetic is the meaning constructed through lived experiences. These meanings include the ways in which we understand identity and community but they are most importantly body meanings; "felt in one's bones." At the micro-level, experience becomes when the individual is attuned to what is happening with her body, when she acknowledges the struggles and joys that constitute her life, and when she uses her imagination or her creative forces to make sense of those experiences. When meaning is given to experience, an aesthetic moment has occurred and an individual, or something about that individual, is appreciated in some way. Burying a son or daughter, an accident resulting in injury, the anticipation of waiting for one's first power wheelchair, sexual desire or pleasure, all become opportunities for aesthetic moments or opportunities for making meaning out of life. Sometimes the meanings are tragic, as when a parent loses a child. And sometimes the meanings are joyful or climactic. If meaning is present, though, the experience is an aesthetic one and life becomes art.

Though embodied, the aesthetic is grounded and visible in a much larger context; a socio-cultural embodiment, of sorts, wherein experience is interpreted through what Hannah Arendt (1978) refers to as the "web of human relations" and what I have counter-argued is the "web of relations" (2002). Arendt's basic position is that humans find meaning in relation to other humans. For example, I give meaning to myself as a mother through my relations with other women, my children, and my husband; and others construct the concept of "mother" as a result of eons of human relations and view me as "mother" in connection with those eons. I understand myself as white, female, mother, wife, and disabled—and others understand me as such or otherwise—through broad cultural processes that move almost unseen through the social world. In contrast, my position is that our lives *also* become meaningful in relation to the nonhuman world; thus, the "web of *relations.*" In this sense, while relations with other humans are important and even crucial, interactions with the nonhuman world also construct lived experience (e.g., whether I walk or wheel up to my workplace, whether there is an elevator or accessible toilet when I need one, whether I can move about the world with or without physical assistance, whether I can lift my face and feel the sun on it or I have to wait for someone to lift it for me, whether my body jerks uncontrollably or lies limp and unmoving or moves in ways I ask it to move).

Incorporating the influence of the web of relations into the aesthetic, it evolves into a collective embodiment that is contingent on what is happening in the nonhuman world, as well as the social processes that flow through bodies as they move in the world. Here I used "body" to represent both the bodies of individuals and the social body comprised of people who share experiences or perspectives to the extent that they share general orientations or standpoints toward those experiences.

Finally, this aesthetic of disability holds the transformative promise of praxis or revolution; a macro-aesthetic. It is a subversive discourse that confronts oppressive social reality and converts it into something liberatory. Like the Brazilian literacy project of Paulo Freire, the "hysterical" females of the Victorian era, and the Latino murals or gang graffiti, an aesthetic of disability forces a confrontation about oppressive social processes using varied strategies (e.g., using the above examples, Freire's strategy was liberatory pedagogy, and hysterical Victorian women had a break from women's work when they became hysterical).

Examples of an Aesthetic of Disability

Examples of an aesthetic of disability are illustrative of the various forms of the aesthetic. Among South Asian Indian-American immigrants who are Hindu, even those who have been in the US for many years, there is often a strong connection to India and Hinduism as they practiced it in India (Gabel et. al., 2001; Gabel, 2004). *Sundar* (Soon-duhr), the mother of an adult daughter labeled profoundly mentally retarded, uses the idea of rebirth (reincarnation) as a way of making sense of her daughter's condition and the meaning of their relationship. "I think she was my mother in a previous life and now she comes back to give to me the problems I gave to her," *Sundar* said when asked for an explanation of her daughter's label. "If she was not my mother, then she was my sister or brother. She is teaching me the lessons I did not learn in my previous body." *Karma* is the Hindu notion of good deeds that reveal lessons learned and that, when completely learned, give release from rebirth. This is the process to which *Sundar* is referring. In contrast to the Western view of disability-as-deficit, and in contrast to the Hindu notion that disability is the result of sin (bad *karma*), *Sundar* embraces her daughter's difference as having an educative purpose by connecting it to past lives they both might have lived. She constructs her own explanatory narrative that is grounded in Indian embodiment and the notion that she will "take several bodies" before she learns all of life's lessons. Rather than seeing her daughter as punishment for past sins, *Sundar* believes her daughter is a gift from god that will help her in this and future lives. *Sundar's* response, though expressed as an individual mother, was formed from within the context of a larger community: South Asian Indians, Hindus, American immigrants, mothers of disabled children. In *Sundar's* story, we find resistance to strong religious and cultural meta-narratives and the construction of the meaning of disability from lived experience and both through the eyes of a nondisabled individual.

Susan Peters, Alan Klein, and Catherine Shadwick (1998) illustrate an aesthetic of disability in their work with urban high school students labeled "learning disabled." Over time, and with engagement in Freirean literacy methods and critical pedagogy, their students formed resistant identities in opposition to the assigned identity "learning disabled." Peters et. al. write that

> The first metaphor characterizes students as *street-wise philosophers* trying to make sense of learning disability and its influence on their lives in school. The second metaphor sees students as *image-makers* who manage the double image of how others see them in relation to their own view of learning disability. The third metaphor takes music as its

> central theme, viewing students...as *jazz improvisationists* in the quest
> for translating the dirge of special education status into a flexible song
> script with an upbeat tempo. (105, emphases added)

Here is an example of disabled students' collective resistance, and of researchers utilizing aesthetic discourse to disrupt dominant values and interpret what they have seen in their field of interaction. The students' aesthetic of disability was formed through life at the margins of school power relations (Bar on's marginal aesthetics) and represented a collective understanding of being assigned the learning disability identity in their school context.

Broad social movements can be interpreted as embedding aesthetic discourse. The Society for Disability Studies' (SDS) decision to use a name whose acronym would recall Students for a Democratic Society, an organization formed in the US in the 1960s to protest the Vietnam War, comes to mind. As a nonprofit organization legally barred from direct political action, SDS used the reference to a former organization as symbolic representation to convey its political orientation. So does Simi Linton's (1998) reference to the civil rights movement of the 1960s, in which she elicits vivid images of embodiment and those experiences Dewey might say are "felt in one's bones."

> We have come out not with brown woolen lap robes over our withered
> legs or dark glasses over our pale eyes but in shorts and sandals, in
> overalls and business suits, dressed for play and work—
> straightforward, unmasked, and unapologetic. We are, as Crosby, Stills,
> and Nash told their Woodstock audience, letting our "freak flags fly."
> (3)

The emerging visibility of crip culture over the last several decades could be interpreted as expanding the reach of aesthetic discourse. Reference to crip culture brings to mind the things that constitute culture: shared values and beliefs, shared patterns of behavior and other norms, shared linguistic traits, power relations, and representations of culture in art. In "Crip Culture Talks Back," Harlan Hahn notes that a culture always has a type of food associated with it. He jokingly proposes that fast food drive-throughs are the food of crip culture because they do not require customers to get out of their cars. Rather than a joke, however, this is serious illustration of the way in which the "web of relations" that includes the physical world forms an aesthetic of disability.

As with any culture, there are problems within crip culture. For example, crip culture requires membership and has hierarchies, and those who are not obvious members or who fall lower in the crip hierarchy (e.g., cognitively disabled people, people who are invisibly disabled) hold an ambiguous position in social space. As liminal individuals, they are neither integral members of crip culture nor are they integral members of able society. Anne Gere's exploration of in/visibility (chapter 4) illuminates this dilemma.

As mentioned earlier, the aesthetic of disability views the aesthetic as a process of coming to know something, as coming to understand. This process occurs at the collective and individual levels. It inheres within and emerges from embodiment, or lived experience. Viewing "coming to know" something as an aesthetic process allows for the kind of play, fluidity, imagination, and permeability that nonaesthetic notions of knowledge processes may not allow. The aesthetic is nonscientific not antiscientific. It offers an alternative way of understanding discourses that create and recreate society and self.

Implications for Research

The aesthetic of disability can be used in multiple ways. Two examples are given here. First, the aesthetic is a theoretical framework within which disability is studied, and second, it is a methodological tool. As a theoretical framework, an aesthetic of disability creates the foundation from which disability can be explored in context, particularly in its contribution to the conceptual tools utilized by the aesthetic: resistance aesthetics, marginal or dominant aesthetics, hegemonic and counter-hegemonic aesthetics, group or collective aesthetics, subversive and transgressive aesthetics. As such, it propels research forward in a search for aesthetic meaning and the ways in which disabled and nondisabled people come to know what it means to "be disabled/human." The aesthetic lens has width and depth. It is inter-disciplinary, therefore it embraces social scientific and humanistic views. It values individual and collective experience, therefore it celebrates "self," "other," and "we" while it also blurs the distinctions between these constructs. It relishes diversity, therefore it encourages a variety of forms of expression and meaning making.

As an interpretive methodological tool, the aesthetic opens up possibilities and creates spaces for interpretation that might not be available without the aesthetic framework. While resistance, marginal and dominant positions, subversion and transgression are used in other theoretical frameworks, interpreting through the aesthetic encourages the search for aesthetic forms of these acts: metaphor and other forms of symbolic representation, narratives, performances, etc. Aesthetic questions asked of one's inquiry texts or "data" are framed quite differently than are non-aesthetic ones (e.g., How are my participants coming to know disability and humanity through embodiment, resistance, perspective, experience, etc.? What forms of expression are being used to convey the meanings associated with and assigned to disability?). And finally, the aesthetic elevates intuition, creativity, and imagination as important processes for inquiry

Aesthetic discourse encourages disability studies to resist itself. It allows Anita Silvers (2002) to suggest, counter-hegemonic to the standard disability studies argument, that rather than serving as a symbol of all that is wrong with humanity, disability offers a way of understanding what is good about humanity: persistence through frailty, the inevitable resistance to power, self- and cultural expression through symbolic act, embodiment, art, creativity, possibilities.

To conclude, Ian Hunter (1992) claims that the aesthetic belongs in the ethical domain. For the individual, the aesthetic is a

> distinctive way of actually conducting one's life—as a self-supporting ensemble of techniques and practices for problematizing conduct and events and bringing oneself into being as the subject of an aesthetic existence. (348)

For collective experience, I would argue similarly; that the aesthetic offers a way of considering group life and that it provides us with the beginnings from which to investigate and understand disability in context.

References

Alcoff, L., and Potter, E. (1992). Introduction: When feminisms intersect epistemology. In L. Alcoff and E. Potter (Eds.), *Feminist epistemologies: Thinking gender* (pp. 1–14). New York: Routledge.

Arendt, H. (1978). *The life of the mind volume I (thinking)*. New York: Harcourt Brace Jovanovich.

Armstrong, I. (2000). *The radical aesthetic*. Oxford, UK: Blackwell Publishers, Ltd.

Bar on, B. A. (1992). Marginality and epistemic privilege. In L. Alcoff and E. Potter (Eds.), *Feminist epistemologies: Thinking gender* (pp. 83–100). New York: Routledge.

Beardsley, M. (1958/81). *Aesthetics: Problems in the philosophy of criticism.* Indianapolis, IN: Hackett Publishing Company, Inc.

Brand, P. Z. (1995). Revising the aesthetic-non-aesthetic distinction: The aesthetic value of activist art. In P. Z. Brand & C. Korsmeye (Eds.), *Feminism and tradition in aesthetics* (pp. 245–72). University Park: Pennsylvania State University Press.

Dewey, J. (1934). *Art as experience.* New York: Berkley Publishing Group.

——— (1926). *Experience and nature.* Chicago: Open Court Publishing Company.

——— (1906/1977). Essays on the new empiricism 1904-06. In J. A. Boydston (Ed.), The middle works of John Dewey, volume 3. Carbondale: Southern Illinois University Press.

Gabel, S., Vyas, S., Patel, H., & Patel, S. (2001). Problems of conceptual translation in cross-cultural disability studies: A South Asian immigrant example. In B. Altman and S. Barnartt (Eds.), *Exploring theories and expanding methodologies: Where we are and where we need to go* (pp. 209–28). Oxford, UK: Elsevier Science Ltd.

Gabel, S. (2004). South Asian cultural orientations toward mental retardation. *Mental Retardation 42,* 12-25.

Gabel, S. (2002a). Some conceptual problems with critical pedagogy. *Curriculum Inquiry,* 32(2), 177–201.

——— (1997). A theory of an aesthetic of disability (Unpublished doctoral dissertation, Michigan State University).

hooks, b. (1990). *Teaching to transgress: Education as the practice of freedom.* New York: Routledge.

Hunter, I. (1992). Aesthetics and cultural studies. In L. Grossberg, C. Nelson, & P. Treicher (Eds.), *Cultural Studies* (pp. 347–67). New York: Routledge.

Jackson, P. (2002). Dewey's 1906 definition of art. *Teachers College Record 104,* 167-77.

Linton, S. (1998). *Claiming disability: Knowledge and identity.* New York: New York University Press.

Marcuse, H. (1978). The *aesthetic dimension: Toward a critique of Marxist aesthetics.* Boston: Beacon Press.

Mitchell, D., & Snyder, S. (1997). Introduction: Disability studies and the double bind of representation. In D. Mitchell and S. Snyder (Eds.), *The body and physical difference: Discourses of disability* (pp. 1–34). Ann Arbor: University of Michigan Press.

Peters, S., Klein, A., & Shadwick, C. (1998). From our voices: Special education and the 'alter-eagle' problem. In B. Franklin (Ed.), *When children don't learn: Student failure and the culture of teaching* (pp. 99–115). New York: Teachers College Press.

Silvers, A. (2002). The crooked timber of humanity: Disability, ideology and the aesthetic. In M. Corker & T. Shakespeare (Eds.), *Disability/postmodernity: Embodying disability theory* (pp. 228–44). London/New York: Continuum.

Simpson, D. (Producer), & Golfus, B. (Director). (1994). *When billy broke his head…and other tales of wonder.* (Documentary). St. Paul, MN: National Awareness Disability Project, Inc., Independent Television.

Snyder, S., & Mitchell, D. (2004). *Self preservation: The art of Riva Lehrer* (documentary). Chicago: Brace Yourself Productions.

3 Disability Arts and the Performance of Ideology

Julie Allan

In recent debates on inclusion, ideology has become a weapon for the denouncement of one group by another. This misses the point, of course, that "ideology is always, by definition, *ideology of ideology*...there is no ideology that does not assert itself by means of delimiting itself from another *mere ideology*" (Zizek, 1994, 19). Brantlinger (qtd. in Zizek, 1994) highlights the importance of "using ideology" (425) in debates on inclusion and to "optimistically keep an eye on the prize in everyday actions" (449), without holding to a utopian vision of inclusion. This chapter responds to Brantlinger's challenge and to Ballard's (1999) call for a debate around the concepts and ideologies that guide policy and practice. Disability studies, the nature of which is being articulated within this book, is centrally concerned with this debate. Disability arts, it is argued here, provides the necessary incitement to the debate, while avoiding some of the pitfalls of ideological critique, and equips us with new forms of discourse to speak against the "culture of silence" (Peters, 1999, 155).

Disability arts represents a powerful new form of ideological critique within disability studies which celebrates difference but also seeks to subvert the "normality genre" (Darke, 1998, 184). Disabled people involved in the production of disability arts use their own bodies as weapons to subvert and undermine disabling barriers and name able-bodied people as part of the problem. This radical genre is driven by pride, beauty, and the celebration of difference, giving disabled people a voice, while also ensuring that their voice is not valorized at the margins (Ram, 1993; Singh, 1995). This chapter examines the work of disabled writers, poets, and musicians. It is argued that their work, which has strong parallels with that of Eastern European writers such as Kundera, Kafka, and Hasek, represents a profound type of ideological critique which forces able-bodied people to confront disabling barriers.

Disability Politics: What's the Use of Ideology?

Disability politics has been characterized recently by a vigorous debate over the place of the body within a social model of disability that seeks to challenge the hegemony of disablism (Oliver, 1996), a process whereby disabled people are systematically excluded from participation in everyday life. The social model, which was developed by disabled people, enables structural, environmental, and attitudinal barriers to be identified and, ideally, removed. The purpose of disability politics has been to fight the able-bodied oppressors and to "win the battle for a social model understanding of society and [disabled people's] lives" (Shakespeare & Watson, 1997, 299). Considerations of individuals' illness or impairment have been regarded as a show of weakness, likely to be seized upon by able-bodied oppressors, but attempts to remove the body from the social model of disability and to privilege unity and consensus over difference have been challenged by writers such as Morris (1991) and Casling (1993). In Kundera's (1986) terms, the removal of the body from the social model amounts to a "rape of privacy" (111) in which disabled people are forced to live a "life without secrets" (110), without their own bodies.

Ideology, Eagleton (1994) reminds us, is a "realm of negotiation, in which there is a constant busy traffic: meaning and values are stolen, transformed, appropriated across the frontiers of different classes and groups, surrendered, repossessed, reinflected" (187). Even so, its function as a type of unmasking is inevitably limited by the metaphysical problem of standing outside the process. The vast range of critiques of ideology has taken us no closer to pinning it down, no nearer to exposing its falsity. At the same time it appears to have transformed into something that is even more unknowable and which tempts us still further into the "trap that makes us slide into ideology under the guise of stepping out of it" (Zizek, 1994, 17). We cannot abandon ideology because it continues to shape what we think we know; but neither can we grasp it in its essence: "Like the poor," writes Eagleton, "ideology is always with us" (1994, 220).

The construct of hegemony has been useful to writers such as Oliver (1990; 1996), Shakespeare (1994), and Vernon (1998), in analyzing the effects of normalization. Abberley (1995) has employed to good effect Thomson's (1984) model of examining "the way in which creative imaginary activities serve to sustain social relations which are asymmetrical with regard to the organisation of power" (6). Abberley's analysis illustrates how the ideology of partnership and the "holistic" approach to occupational therapy work to sustain notions of disability as an individual problem. He also demonstrates how this enables blame for the failure of therapy to be placed upon the clients rather than the professionals. Imrie's (1998) analysis of the ideology of architecture suggests that the perpetuation of ablist and masculine values contributes to the oppression faced by disabled people, while Peters (1999) has illustrated how disabled people buy into the "culture of silence" (103) and accept the labels which construct them as "passive recipients in welfare-oriented societies" (103). The marginalization which ensues is absolute (Mairs, 1996), so that disabled people "embody the metaphors" of marginality, occupying a "physical space literally outside the field of vision of those in the center" (Mairs, 1996, 59).

A more sinister deployment of ideology is its use as a weapon against those holding opposing views. Special education "traditionalists" (Brantlinger, 1997, 430) such as Fuchs and Fuchs (1994) have accused inclusionists of deriving their ideas (merely) from ideology and of being inclined to "misinterpret research findings for ideological reasons" (Kavale, Fuchs, & Scruggs, 1994, 77). Kauffman (1995) has voiced his concerns for the educational welfare of children, which he sees as under threat from the ideology of the inclusionists: "Full inclusion ideology seems to imply that the congregation of students in neighbourhood schools for general education purposes is sacrosanct" (229). There are two observations to make here, the first of which is to reemphasize the impossibility of speaking from outside ideology: "[A]ny criticism of another's views as ideological is always susceptible to a swift *tu quoque.* In pulling the rug out from beneath one's intellectual antagonist, one is always in danger of pulling it out from beneath oneself" (Eagleton, 1994, 193).

Brantlinger suggests that the traditionalists might have a case if they were to accuse inclusionists of "idealism or demagoguery," but their pejorative depictions of the ideology of others is based on an ignorance "which cannot be excused as benign" (Brantlinger, 1997, 436).

The second observation concerns the reduction of the debate to a limited form of "stunted reflexivity" (Gouldner, 1976, 48). Foucault (1984) asserts that ideology "cannot be used without circumspection" (60) because its suggestion of false consciousness, the privileging of reality over ideology and the possibility of "true" knowledge (Cooper, 1997) compromises its analytical possibilities. Even so, that act of circumspection forces us to endure a series of "metaphysical phantasies" (Pêcheux, 1994, 150) in which ideology appears for what it is not: "[A] noble and vague style, apt for idealizing practices while appearing to describe them. Ideology is an ample cloak that dissimulates the crooked and dissimilar contours of the real practices that succeed one another in history" (Veyne, 1997, 156). Zizek (1994) suggests we are further compromised by our current existence in the society of the spectacle. That is, our perceptions of reality are structured by a serious of aesthetizised images of it through the media and advertising. Furthermore, Kundera (1991) argues that ideology has been replaced by a more powerful and omnipresent "imagology," which functions "to create truth, the most democratic truth that ever existed" (Kundera, 1991, 128), but in image only. Thus, "the wheels of imagology turn without having any effect upon history" (Kundera, 1991, 129).

Ideology has been denounced as self-defeating, useless and premised on a misrecognition of social reality (Zizek, 1994). Its uselessness is particularly galling to Rorty (1994) who argues that "all that matters is what we can do to persuade people to act differently than in the past" (231). However, as Zizek (1994) observes, it is this practicization of ideology which has obscured our understanding of it as a concept. Ideological critique, in seeking to become respectable as theory, has lost its identity as satire and as a consequence has closed down avenues for dialogue rather than opening them up. Sloterdijk suggests that this has also forced it to become entangled in dogma and radical solutions such as psychopathology: "False consciousness appears first of all as sick consciousness" (19). Paradoxically, the act of unpicking some of the obscurities in ideology, and helping to recover its sense of humor, could possibly alert us to its more productive possibilities and put it to work more effectively.

Derrida's (1998) criticisms of ideology were based on what he saw as its historical limitations. Nevertheless, he considered it to have potential, providing certain relationships are taken into account. The relation of the ideological to the scientific is crucial, according to Derrida, but this has largely been ignored. One notable exception is Gallagher's (1998) analysis of the scientific basis of special education in which she questions the knowledge we think we have within this field. The relation of the ideological to the philosophical is also important, yet much neglected, leading Derrida to question the logic of claims to a theory of ideology. Finally, Derrida argues that ideology needs to be connected with an examination of the problematics of language and the science of writing.

Derrida's spectral analysis (1998) helps us to navigate the impossibility of distinguishing the real from the ideological, by suggesting that reality never appears itself, but always through spectral apparitions. These specters cannot uncover the real because they fill up the hole left by it. Put another way, they make up part of what is real, and so by taking it away, what is assumed to be real would be incomplete. While this appears helpful, insofar as it enables us to search for the ghosts or specters which materialize, rather than the "spiritual, substanceless big Other of ideology" (Zizek, 1994, 20) it does not offer, as Zizek suggests, a "pre-ideological kernel" (20). Rather, it offers us a more tangible grasp of what we are unable to see: "The specter *appears* to present itself during its visitation. One represents it to oneself, but it is not present, itself, in flesh and blood" (Derrida, 1998, 145; original emphasis). Furthermore, the specter "first of all sees us" (45) rendering us anxious, but nevertheless attentive to a variety of reversals such as presence/absence; ghost/non-ghost; real/unreal. Derrida argues that rather than demanding the real presence of a specter or chasing it away, the scholar must learn from the ghost in the way that Shakespeare's Mercellus enjoined Horatio in Hamlet: "Thou art a scholar; speak to it Horatio. ... question it" (cited in Derrida, 1998, 163). Derrida suggests that the scholar should learn "how to talk with him, with her, how to let them speak or how to give them back speech, even if it is in oneself, in the other, in the other in oneself: they are always *there*, specters, even if they do not exist, even if they are no longer, even if they are not yet" (163).

Zizek (1994) argues that far from being a useless construct, ideology has taken on a greater importance. Rather than seek to pin down the essence of ideology and our relationship to it, we should seek to obfuscate and estrange ourselves from it:

> Herein lies one of the tasks of the "postmodern" critique of ideology: to designate the elements within an existing social order which—in the guise of "fiction," that is of "Utopian" narratives of possible but failed alternative histories—point towards the system's antagonistic character, and thus *estrange* us to the self-evidence of its established identity. (7; original emphasis)

He suggests that what seems like an impasse can be viewed as a productive insider/outsider space, in which "[i]deology is not all; it is possible to assume a place that enables us to maintain a distance from it, *but this place from which one can denounce ideology must remain empty, it cannot be occupied by any positively determined reality*—the moment we yield to this temptation, we are back in ideology" (17; original emphasis). In this space splitting takes place, offering a series of oppositions (for example between state and market, society and self), which allows us both to see and not see ideology by observing how those very oppositions unravel themselves. Ideology, once it becomes a cultural performance, goes limp.

Ideology as an Art Form

Disability arts seeks to "strategically deploy *difference* in order to make a political difference" (Singh, 1995, 197) and involves individuals portraying themselves as aesthetic objects, through dance, photography, art, and other cultural forms. It performs a dual function:

> Disability arts also provides a context in which disabled people can get together, enjoy themselves and think in some way about issues of common concern. But it goes deeper than that as a disability culture really does offer a key into the basic process of identifying as a disabled person, because culture and identity are closely linked concepts. (Vasey, 1992, 11)

A major impetus for disability arts is the rejection of the invisibility imposed upon them. For example, Sue Napolitano's *My Place*, placed at the front of a UK consultation document on arts and disability policy describes her desire not to be hidden away in "bungalow land," but to live instead in the "pulse-hot-thick of it" (McLean, 1998). A number of writers set out to subvert "the normality genre" (Darke, 1998, 184) and to discomfit able-bodied people, by forcing them to examine their own normalizing and disablist attitudes. This writing features prominently in the growing literature on disability studies texts (e.g., Davis, 1997; Mitchell & Snyder, 1997) and on Internet sites such as *Cripzine*, a magazine devoted to promoting disability arts and culture and *Not Dead Yet*. It unravels the *politically correct* language of disability, using words like cripple and freak in ways that are both affirming and excluding. Mairs (1986), for example, describes herself as a "cripple," precisely because "people—crippled or not —wince at the word." She wants people to see her as someone who can "face the brutal truth of her experience squarely: As a cripple I swagger" (9). She also sets out deliberately to write, not just about the body, but "as a body" (1996, 60), and it is this aspect which she thinks distinguishes her work (or rather exiles it) from conventional academic discourse: "(...the guys may be writing with the pen/penis, but they pretend at all times to keep it in their pants). And it is this—my—crippled female body that my work struggles to redeem through that most figurative of human tools: language" (1996, 60). Mairs argues that her work is doomed to failure—"because language substitutes a no-thing for a thing, whereas a body is a pure thing through and through" (1996, 60). She may, however, be underestimating the depths reached by her ideological critique.

The following poem by Wade (1987) performs her marginalized experience.

I am not one of the
I am not one of the physically challenged—

I'm a sock in the eye with a gnarled fist
I'm a French kiss with cleft tongue
I'm orthopedic shoes sewn on a last of your fears

I am not one of the differently abled—

I'm an epitaph for a million imperfect babies left untreated
I'm an icon carved from bones in a mass grave in
Tiergarten, Germany—
I'm withered legs hidden with a blanket

I am not one of the able disabled—

I'm a black panther with green eyes and scars like a picket fence
I'm pink lace panties teasing a stub of milk white thigh
I'm the Evil Eye

I'm the first cell divided
I'm mud that talks
I'm Eve I'm Kali
I'm The Mountain That Never Moves
I've been forever I'll be here forever
I'm the Gimp
I'm the Cripple
I'm the Crazy Lady

I'm the Woman With Juice
(Cheryl Marie Wade, quoted in Davis, 1997).

Wade reverses beauty and ugliness, portraying herself as both a sexual object—with lace panties—and as deformed—with a stub—and demands a presence which has been denied through notions of being "physically challenged," by asserting that she will be "here forever." She asserts her sexual and gendered identities in playful ways that challenge the desexing discourses of disability (Allan, 1999). Wade also provides an unassailable argument by presenting both itself *and its opposition*, unity and difference, ugliness and beauty, leaving nothing to contest. This playful irony disturbs in the way that Kundera (1986) suggests the truly great novel irritates—"not because it mocks or attacks but because it denies us our certainties by unmasking the world as an ambiguity" (134).

The work of Audre Lorde provides a further example of writing by "powerful women" (Thomson, 1997, 240) who have embraced their liminality as black disabled women and foregrounded their difference. Lorde pursues a form of byomythography, an revisionist narrative of self as *Zami*, in which a cluster of excluding and affirming attributes—"fat, Black, nearly blind and ambidextrous" (1982, 240) frees her up from normalizing and assimilating conventions, so that her very distinctiveness becomes the site of power and politics.

> The marked women inspire awe at the profusion of difference their bodies flaunt, challenging the supposedly superior status of normalcy by rendering it banal. These literary representations accentuate the marked body's historical context, infusing the material body with social meaning rather than metaphorical significance. By connecting physical being with individual history and culture, the extraordinary women figures define the self in terms of its uniqueness rather than its conformity to the norm. (Thomson, 1997, 261)

The abnormal body thus becomes sanctioned as a means of disrupting the unity and order of its opposite, and exposing it in all its banality (Thomson, 1997, 261). Even so, it is risky activity because of the danger of provoking contempt and the double bind that "we fear the visibility without which we could truly live and that the visibility which make us most vulnerable is also the source of our greatest strength" (Lorde, 42).

Turning to song, the lyrics of Johnny Crescendo, a British singer, explores a number of themes. Some of these are explicitly political, with lines like "you gotta fight for your rights"; "not dead yet"; and in one entitled "Fixed Penalty," Crescendo makes his demands clear:

> Access access don't segregate
> No cripple free zone
> And no apartheid
> Access access no shut gate
> What we want is access now
>
> Access access there's laws being passed
> To take us out of circulation
> Put us out to grass
> We won't take this and we're gonna kick ass
> What we want is access now

One song offers a seriously playful retake on the nursery rhyme "the wheels of the bus go round, but we can't get on the bus," while another, entitled "Suit scared," explores the singer's "cultural confusion" and asks "that if we have a disability culture why do we wear non disabled suits?" All of these songs make it clear that it is the able-bodied who need to do the thinking and changing, but the "Ballad of Josie Evans" spells this out even more forcefully:

Ballad of Josie Evans
Josie was a wheelchair user spent 11 years inside
A short stay institution where she was banged up without trial
11 years the white coats met and talked and analysed
Dispensed the drugs politely until one day Josie died

Not me said the social worker I was Josie's friend
She was our best customer I was with her till the end
Our boss said no resources were available at the time
And I'm just an employee can't put my job on the line

Not me said the director I can't be held to blame
It's the politicians who make decisions I'm just a pawn in their game
I agree most strongly that Ms Evans was done wrong
But the Council wanted cuts and I had to sing their song

And the finger of guilt draws a circle in the sand
And who'll take the blame for the desperate and the dammed
And which people vote for injustice in the land
Is it you or your mother is it you...

Josie left a letter which I found amongst her things
It said I am and I survive and my heart still has wings
They can take away my freedom
They can drug me with their lies
But they don't have my permission
And I hang onto my pride

Each of these artists *perform*, rather than seek to expose, ideology and take us to the heart of disabling practices, providing a "problem solving framework" (Biklin, 2000, 341) in which "others must participate" (Mairs, 1996, p71). Their work can be read as a particularly effective form of ideological critique which (Sloterdijk, 1987) has termed kynicism and this, together with the parallels with the writing by Eastern European novelists, is explored below.

Kynicism and Performative Ideology

Kynicism, an ancient Greek form of "pantomimic argument," seeks to make ideology limp and, by so doing, puts it to work in a productive way. It is similar to the strategy of disidentifcation described by Pêcheux (1994), in which individuals work antagonistically on or against the prevailing practices of ideological subjection, so that identifications are displaced. It succeeds, not by triumphing over ideology in any confrontational sense, but in forcing ideology to do its own unraveling. It is entirely different from the cynicism employed in versions of ideological critique in which the cynic understands the distance between the ideological mask and the social reality, but still insists on the mask: "[T]hey know very well what they are doing, but still they are doing it" (Zizek, 1994, 312). The problem with cynicism as enlightened false consciousness, according to Sloterdijk (1987), is that it has become, "a hard-boiled shadowy cleverness that has split courage off from itself, holds anything positive to be fraud, and is intent on somehow getting through life. He who laughs last, laughs as if in pleural shock" (546).

Kynicism, in contrast, uses subversive tactics to confront the pathetic phrases of the ruling ideology. It mocks solemnity through banality and ridicule, but does so by pragmatic, rather than argumentative, means. More precisely, its argument is pantomimic—lived rather than spoken—and inspired by cheekiness. Sloterdijk's account suggests it requires a level of outrageousness, "pissing against the idealist wind" (103), to achieve its disruptive goals:

> Ancient kynicism begins the process of *naked arguments* from the opposition, carried by the power that comes from below. The kynic farts, shits, pisses, masturbates on the street, before the eyes of the Athenian market. He shows contempt for fame, ridicules the architecture, refuses respect, parodies the stories of gods and heroes.... (Sloterdijk, 1987, 103)

Kynicism appears to succeed where ideological critique does not, in breaking the "structure of cares" (Heidegger, cited in Sloterdijk, 1987, 124) and attacking the piety of seriousness through the "physiologically irresistible energy of laughter" (Sloterdijk, 1987, 110). This form of critique is particularly embodied in that bodies are used as weapons as the following example from Sloterdijk illustrates. In 1969, Adorno was prevented from giving a lecture by demonstrators, among them some women, who attracted his attention by baring their breasts. Sloterdijk suggests that the women were using their bodies as weapons of critique, and achieving "praxis as social change" (109) and argues that this was more effective than other forms of challenge. Kynicism, thus, is promoted as a kind of "healthy narcissism" (127) and self-affirmation which sets out to "laugh in the face of the impudent demands of such morose societies" (Sloterdijk, 1987, 127). This form of activity seems to form the basis of much of the writing by disabled people.

Kynicism has also been given a voice by nondisabled Eastern European writers in the space of the novel. According to Kundera (1986), the greatness of the novel as a form lies not in its potential to capture the essence of humanity, but to explore the possibilities of human experience. Kafka's exaggeration of the bureaucracy and the fate of individuals in it articulates the fantasy that creates our own belief in the "almightiness" (Zizek, 1994, 318) of bureaucratic realities. Zizek suggests that this is a particularly persuasive form of ideological analysis because, rather than get at the essence of the ideological form itself, Kafka lets us explore the efficiency of the fantasy in our social reality. The novels of the Eastern Europeans adopt a form of kynicism which takes us to the "horror of the comic" where we are inside the "guts of a joke" (Kundera, 1986, 104), rather than looking at it from the outside. It is from this place, however, that we come to understand Ionesco's observation that "there is a thin line between the horrible and the comic" (quoted in Kundera, 1986, 136).

Hasek (1973) takes us to the horror of the comic through the eyes of the *Good Soldier Svejk* and his long-suffering Lieutenant Lukàs. His characters experience a kind of misrecognition of the other, with the Lieutenant becoming more and more frustrated at Svejk's apparent stupidity: "There was no sign of anger in his pale face. There was just hopelessness and desperation," (473) while Svejk tries hard to learn from past encounters: "Humbly report, sir, it's a very long story and you are always pleased to get angry when I go into a lot of detail. Like the time you wanted to hit me over the jaw…" (Hasek, 1973, 471). At the end of one such exchange, "Svejk got solemnly into his van. He felt respect for himself. It did not happen everyday that he committed something so frightful that he must never be allowed to learn what it was" (476).

The misrecognition between the two is both horrible and comical because, as Gogol suggests, "the longer and more carefully we look at a funny story, the sadder it becomes" (cited in Kundera, 1986, 136). The brutal meaningless of war, and of human experience, is foregrounded in the characters' conversations, but this unraveling is so profoundly idiotic that we must also laugh, as a kind of empty consolation. Kundera suggests that the art of the novel came into being, following Rabelais, as the echo of God's laughter: "Because man thinks and the truth escapes him" (158). Rabelais feared what he termed agélastes, who could not laugh, who thought the truth is obvious and who were convinced of certainty. Both the novel and the work of the disabled artists have a great deal to say about ideology and about those who cannot laugh at the limitations of their own thinking.

Disability arts goes further in requiring nondisabled people to recognize the ways in which they are implicated in disability and to learn how to change.

The form of kynicism employed by disabled people is hard to take, because it is so raunchy and "in your face." It is also difficult to make judgments about, both as an art form and as ideological critique. The "horror of the comic" (Kundera, 1986, 104) and the impossibilities experienced by characters portrayed by Kafka, Hasek, Kunder,a and others provoke in the reader a mixture of surprise and relief, along with a "clear implication that laughter is life's exception" (Stronach & Allan, 1999). Even though, where disabled people are concerned, this laughter immediately renders us self-conscious and places us back within the "call of care" (Heidegger, cited in Sloterdijk, 1987, 417), where we judge such a response as inappropriate and disrespectful. Its effectiveness as a form of ideological critique, through its questioning of normalizing and disabling ideology, is evident. As an approach that aspires to make ideology limp without ever promising to expose it, but which also forces able-bodied people to confront their own banality, to laugh at their stupidity and to recognize how this disables, it is more spirited and possibly more productive than other forms of analysis: "Only the greatest impudence still has words for reality. Only anarchic waywardness still finds an expression of contemporary normality" (Sloterdijk, 1987, 546).

Openings for Disability Arts?

Disability studies represents a call for "reimaginings of disability" (Ware, 2001, 109) and the early responses to this in writing, which can be located within frameworks of poststructuralism/postmodernism (Gabel, 1998, 2001) and critical pedagogy (Peters, 1999; Erevelles, 2000) are very promising indeed. Disability arts, with its emphasis on performing, rather than exposing, ideology is an important element within disability studies and the playful and disruptive boundary work of the performers must be encouraged. More importantly, the exposure of a deeply complacent and suspicious education community to this genre could help its members to get the point about inclusion—finally. Ware (2001) cautions us about the tensions around "attempting to consider disability as a concept or a constituency in educational settings" (107), but Peters (1999) reminds us that young disabled people are much more than the passive labels they accept and embody. They are also, she contends, "street wise philosophers, image makers and jazz improvisationists" (114), who, in spite of the psychological violence done to their images in schools, succeed in making their own music:

What students are asking for is learning that has a regular beat, but a faster tempo and which improvises while maintaining harmony. Essentially this requires a musical script where no part is left out, but solos are encouraged, and the range of octaves is unlimited. They want school to be a jazz session: creative, challenging, spiritual, collectively harmonized. (115)

Inclusion as music making? Now that's what I call art.

References

Abberley, P. (1995). Disabling ideology in health and welfare—The case of occupational therapy. *Disability and Society, 10*(2), 221–236.

Allan, J. (1999). *Actively seeking inclusion.* London: Falmer.

Ballard, K., Ed. (1999). Concluding thoughts. In K. Ballard (Ed.), *Inclusive education: International voices on disability and justice.* London: Falmer.

Brantlinger, E. (1997). Using ideology: Cases of nonrecognition of the politics of research and practice in special education. *Review of Educational Research, 67*(4), 425–459.

Casling, D. (1993). Cobblers and song-birds: The language and imagery of disability. *Disability, Handicap and Society, 8*(2), 199–206.

Cooper, D. (1997). Strategies of power: Legislating worship and religious education. In M. Lloyd & A. Thacker (Eds.), *The impact of Michel Foucault on the social sciences and the humanities.* Basingstoke: MacMillan Press.

Crescendo, J. Web site http://206.244.52/.

Cripzine: Disability Arts and Culture. Web site http://www.stanford.edu/-jarron/crip.htm.

Darke, P. (1998). Understanding cinematic representations of disability. In T. Shakespeare (Ed.), *The disability reader: Social science perspectives.*

Davis, L. (Ed.). (1997). *The disability studies reader.* London: Routledge.

Derrida, J. (1998). Specters of Marx. In J. Wolfreys (Ed.), *The Derrida reader.* Edinburgh: Edinburgh University Press.

Eagleton, T. (1994). Ideology and its vicissitudes in western Marxism. In S. Zizek (Ed.), *Mapping ideology.* London: Verso.

Erevelles, N. (2000). Educating unruly bodies: Critical pedagogy, disability studies and the politics of schooling. *Educational Theory, 50*(1), 25–47.

Foucault, M. (1984). Truth and method. In P. Rabinow (Ed.), *The Foucault reader.* Harmondsworth: Penguin.

Fuchs, D., & Fuchs, L. (1994). Inclusive schools movement and the radicalization of special education reform. *Exceptional Children, 60*(4), 294–309.

Gabel, S. (2001). "I wash my face with dirty water": Narratives of disability and pedagogy. *Journal of Teacher Education, 52,* 31–47.

——— (1998). Depressed and disabled: Some discursive problems with mental illness. In M. Crocker & S. French (Eds.), *Disability Discourse.* Buckingham: Open University Press.

Gallagher, D. (1998). The scientific knowledge base of special education: Do we know what we think we know? *Exceptional Children, 64,* 493–502.

Gouldner, A. (1976). *The dialectic of ideology and technology.* New York: Seabury.

Hasek, J. (1973). *The good soldier Sjvek.* Harmondsworth: Penguin.

Imrie, R. (1998). Oppression in the built environment. In T. Shakespeare (Ed.), *The disability reader: Social science perspectives.* London: Cassell.

Kauffman, J. (1995). Why we must celebrate a diversity of restrictive environments. *Learning Disabilities Research and Practice, 10*(4), 225–232.

Kavale, K., Fuchs, D., & Scruggs, T. (1994). Setting the record straight on learning disability and low achievement: Implications for policy making. *Learning Disabilities Research and Practice, 9*(2), 70–77.

Kundera, M. (1991). *Immortality.* London: Faber and Faber.

——— (1986). *The art of the novel.* London: Faber and Faber.

Lorde, A. (1982). *Zami: A new spelling of my name.* Freedom, CA: Crossing Press.

Mairs, N. (1996). *Waist high in the world.* Boston: Beacon.

——— (1986). On being a cripple. *Plaintext: Essays.* Tucson: University of Arizona Press.

McLean, D. (1998). *Beyond barriers: A consultation paper on arts and disability policy.* Web site: http://ndaf.org.Pages/BEYONDBARRIERS

Mitchell, D., & Snyder, S. (1997). (Eds.). *The body and physical difference: Discourses of disability.* Ann Arbor: The University of Michigan Press.

Morris, J. (1991). *Pride against prejudice: Transforming attitudes to disability.* London: The Women's Press.

Oliver, M. (1996). *Understanding disability: From theory to practice.* Basingstoke: Macmillan Press.

——— (1990). *The politics of disablement.* Basingstoke: Macmillan and St. Martin's Press.

Pêcheux, M. (1994). Ideological (mis)recognition. In S. Zizek (Ed.), *Mapping ideology.* London: Verso.

Peters, S. (1999). Transforming disability identity. In M. Corker & S. French (Eds.), *Disability discourse.* Buckingham: Open University Press.

Ram, K. (1993). Too "traditional" once again: Some poststructuralists on the aspirations of the immigrant/third world female subject. *Australian Feminist Studies, 17,* 5–28.

Rorty, R. (1994). Feminism, ideology and deconstruction: A pragmatist view. In S. Zizek (Ed.), *Mapping ideology.* London: Verso.

Shakespeare, T. (1994). Cultural representation of disabled people: Dustbins for disavowal? *Disability and Society, 9*(3), 283–299.

Shakespeare, T., & Watson, N. (1997). Defending the social model, *Disability and Society, 12*(2), 293–300.

Singh, P. (1995). Voicing the "Other," speaking for the "self," disrupting the metanarratives of educational theorizing with poststructural feminism. In K. Smith & P. Wexler (Eds.). *After postmodernism.* London: Falmer.

Sloterdijk, P. (1987). *Critique of cynical reason.* Minneapolis: University of Minnesota Press.

Stronach, I., & Allan, J. (1999). Joking with disability: What's the difference between the comic and tragic in disability discourses? *Body and Society, 5*(4), 31–45.

Thomson, J. (1984). *Studies in the theory of ideology*. Cambridge: Polity Press.

Thomson, R. G. (1997). Disabled women as powerful women in Petry, Morrison and Lorde. In D. Mitchell & S. Snyder (Eds.), *The body and physical difference: Discourses of disability*. Ann Arbor: University of Michigan Press.

Vasey, S. (1992). Disability arts and culture: An introduction to key issues and questions. In S. Lees (Ed.), *Disability arts and culture papers*. London: Shape Publications.

Vernon, A. (1998). Multiple oppression and the disabled people's movement. In T. Shakespeare (Ed.), *The disability reader: Social science perspectives*. London: Cassell.

Veyne, P. (1997). Foucault and his interlocutors. In A. Davidson (Ed.), *Foucault and his interlocutors*. Chicago: University of Chicago Press.

Wade, C. (1987). I am not one of the. In L. Davis (Ed.), *The disability studies reader*. London: Routledge.

Ware, L. (2001). Writing, identity and the other: Dare we do disability studies? *Journal of Teacher Education, 52*(2), 107–123.

Zizek, S. (Ed.). (1994). *Mapping ideology*. London: Verso.

4 Seeing is/not Believing: Visibility, Invisibility, and Disability Studies in Education

Anne Ruggles Gere

It's the first day of the new semester. With a class list, 35 copies of the syllabus, and a new edition of the first text to be read, the instructor walks through the door. S/he scans the half dozen students who have already arrived, noting the pierced eyebrow, the various pigmentations of skin, the day-glo hair gelled into five spikes, the dark eyes glowering under the brim of a baseball cap, and the folded arms of the person sitting in the left rear corner. As others enter the classroom, s/he picks out physical markers that will help tie names on the class list to the bodies that fill the room. When the class moves into the rituals of introductions, roll taking, and course explanations, the instructor continues to read the class, taking notes so automatically it's possible to be almost unaware of them. "The make-up doesn't cover the acne scars of the one in the back. She looks angry." "That guy is painfully thin, and his spine seems curved to the left. I won't have any trouble remembering his name." "She is shorter than everyone in the class. I wonder if she is even five feet tall."

At the same time, students are busy reading the instructor. Their eyes focus on the body: How old is this person? Is this an athlete or a sloth? Is there a ring on the left hand? Are the clothes stylish? They watch gestures: "Does s/he seem receptive or impatient?" The eyes: "Is there kindness or cruelty there?" The mouth: "Is there evidence of a sense of humor?" This first reading of the instructor's body often determines whether individual students drop or add a class; for those who stay this body reading will shape interactions throughout the semester. And for instructors also, visual inspections lead to inferences and assumptions that shape teaching throughout the semester.

The gaze, as Michel Foucault (1975) terms it, dominates the classroom. Drawing on the image of the physician, Foucault describes the gaze as traveling from body to body, focusing on the concrete and sensible. It is a way of seeing that moves past distractions into the truth of things (120). Foucault describes the gaze as a myth of modernity. After the modern age threw off medieval superstition, it created its own myths, and the concept of the gaze as a means of penetrating illusion and discerning hidden truths is one of these. Postmodernism, as defined by Jean-Francois Lyotard (1993), is an incredulity toward metanarratives or grand theories that claim total explanatory power. Part of the project of postmodernism is to interrogate grand theories like the myth of the gaze, and this chapter examines the implications of this myth for pedagogy, research, and epistemology in education.

As the familiar classroom scene demonstrates, the myth of the gaze permeates conventional assumptions about pedagogy. The instructor often believes that visual inspection of student bodies will reveal truths that can inform teaching. Students frequently engage in reciprocal gazing, even though theirs comes from a perspective of unequal power. The teacher, after all, controls the currency of the course grade and has the authority to reward or punish the performances of students. This power infiltrates the instructor's perception, reinforcing the seeming penetration of the gaze and making it difficult to interrogate the myth of the gaze. The teacher's use of the gaze renders it even more powerful. With a raised eyebrow, a glare, a glance of recognition, or a wink, the instructor signals approval, disapproval or permission. Even when students resist these controlling gazes with rolled, averted, or closed eyes, everyone in the classroom assumes that the greater power remains in the teacher's gaze. The headiness of this power can lead the instructor to embrace the myth of the gaze more firmly, believing that the gaze can reveal an underlying reality or a hidden truth about individual students.

Disability studies can inform our thinking about the gaze in the classroom. One of the most important and contested terms in the field of disability studies is visibility. As Brenda Bruggeman (2001) notes, "Disability studies activists and scholars talk and write a lot about 'visibility'" (369). Yet, as one of her students observed, "You've said that several times now—that there are about 56 million Americans with disabilities. Then why don't we ever see any of them?" Bruggeman's answer touches on the myth of the gaze ("Another concern lies in the metaphor of visibility to begin with..."), and it also explores the complex terrain of how invisibility and visibility interact in the classroom. As she puts it, we need to "*see* what is meant by the *invisibility of disability*" (369).

By way of illustration, I'd like you to *see* my daughter Cindy walking into a classroom with her books tucked under one arm. Her straight black hair hangs down her back, and her dark eyes scan the board as she moves gracefully toward a seat near the front. Several of the male students eye her body approvingly; she is very attractive. Throughout this and every other class she is a model student, taking notes diligently and participating in class discussions. If papers are assigned, she will turn in neatly typed pages. If no in-class writing is required, and if she chooses, she can "pass." Her teachers will have no idea how hard she is working or what those neatly typed papers cost her. When teachers do see a page of her unedited handwritten prose, they recoil in horror with exclamations like, "This is illiterate. I can't read a word." or "How did you get this far? What are you doing in college?" When she was younger, I was often the one to hear the teachers' incredulity. Sometimes they would say, having no idea how much labor Cindy put into her often average performance, "If she would just work a little harder…" "I don't think she tries hard enough." More often, they would express disbelief when I explained the tangle of misfiring neurons inside Cindy's head: "I can't believe it. She looks so good."

In the classroom, as in every other area of her life, Cindy is faced with the choice of whether to reveal or conceal her impairment. When she meets someone new she has to decide whether and/or when to tell that person about her limitations. If a new young man enters her life, the decision becomes especially complicated. "Will he still be attracted to me if he knows the 'whole truth' about me?" she wonders. Every interview, every application is a minefield of uncertainties that she must tiptoe through. She has to decide again and again if she will share the fact that she has Fetal Alcohol Syndrome (FAS). Not long ago she, a newly certified art teacher, struggled with this decision yet again. She was applying for a position at a Native American charter school, a job she wanted very badly because it had long been her desire to affirm her own Native American heritage by working with youngsters from the same population. The application contained this line: ""Do you have any mental, physical, or medical impairment or disability that would limit your job performance or require special accommodations to complete the application process or perform the essential functions of the position for which you are applying?"

Everything else on the application was easy, but Cindy deliberated a long time over that question. She lamented: "If I tell them about my FAS, they probably won't hire me. But if I say 'no' and then make some dumb mistake, they'll probably call me a liar and fire me."

As I listened to Cindy, I was reminded of the enormous weight of anxiety and self-doubt her invisible impairment imposes. The "choice" she has does not bring a sense of access or liberation. She is continually challenged and conflicted by having to decide. When she reveals her condition, she frequently encounters disbelief and denial. "No," a new friend or teacher will say, "there must be some mistake. I don't believe you have a disability." Teachers, clinging, I assume, to the myth of the gaze, are especially likely to respond in this way. They actively refuse to believe that she has any impairment. In one of her darker moments, Cindy moaned, "What do I have to do? Show them a CAT scan?" Later she painted a large canvas with a human brain in the center. Half the brain indicated normal connections while the other showed the jagged lines of broken connections. She titled the painting "Living Proof."

Cindy's experience with the teaching application also reminded me of Nella Larsen's novel *Passing* in which Claire Kendry, the central character, abandons her African American roots in order to "pass" as a white woman. She confides one of her greatest fears to a friend: "I nearly died of terror the whole nine months before Margery was born for fear she might be dark. Thank goodness she turned out all right. But I'll never risk it again. Never! The stress is simply too, too hellish" (168). Her white husband, when asked if he dislikes Negroes, responds: "Nothing like that at all. I don't dislike them. I hate them"(p. 172). Claire reconnects with her African American friends, and at the end of the novel her husband discovers her deception and confronts her: "So you're a nigger, a damned dirty nigger" (p.238), and Claire falls or is pushed out the window to her death shortly after. In Cindy's lament I heard the same anxieties about passing, the same fears of being discovered and sent away. But revealing her disability could lead to immediate rejection. She had to choose.

A number of years ago when I was on the faculty at the University of Washington, I passed Husky Stadium as I walked to campus each day. One spring the stadium was being remodeled to add another deck of seats. Each day I watched the progress of the steel girders extending skyward and imagined how the finished structure would look. Weeks passed, and I could see the entire structure outlined against the sky. One morning, after I had passed the stadium and headed uphill toward my office, I heard an enormous crash followed by a succession of smaller clattering sounds. When I looked back I saw that the entire structure had fallen into a tangle of metal. Whenever I think about how Cindy must feel about the consequences of her "choice," that falling stadium rings in my ears. Will her choice to reveal or conceal cause her hopes to come crashing down?

The invisible impairment offers a way of interrogating the myth of the gaze, especially as it functions in pedagogy. Cindy's experiences as a student and the frequent reactions of her teachers suggest how powerfully the myth of the gaze retains its hold in the classroom. As Cindy's experience also demonstrates, the visible is not an accurate measure of the "reality" of another's body. Jacques Lacan (1998) writes, "In this matter of the visible, everything is a trap" (Four Freud Concepts 93), and pedagogy demonstrates that to be visible is to be subject to surveillance and voyeurism. It can be dangerous or at least uncomfortable be visible, especially with an impairment that can be seen. Accordingly, we need to rethink the value of the visible and be cautious about how much credit we give to what we can see.

To question the status of the visible raises, of course, an interesting set of questions. During the past two decades, in concert with the forces of identity politics, disability advocates have emphasized visibility. As Simi Linton (1998) puts it, "Disabled people, and I will immediately identify myself as one, are a group only recently entering everyday civic life...We have come out not with brown woolen lap robes over our withered legs or dark glasses over our pale eyes but in shorts and sandals, in overalls and business suits, dressed for play and work—straight-forward, unmasked and unapologetic" (3). With increased visibility have come significant political advances, including the Americans with Disabilities Act of 1990, which was designed to guarantee the civil rights of people with disabilities.

As I write, however, the U.S. Supreme Court has just voted 5-4 on *University of Alabama v. Garrett*. This case, focused on the right of disabled persons to sue the state for discriminatory treatment, challenges the ADA's constitutionality by ruling that Congress cannot require states to pay money damages for injuries caused when states violate the ADA. In other words, the Supreme Court privileged state sovereignty over the civil rights of individuals with impairments. Brenda Bruggeman (2001) has written this about people with impairments: "And it is only in often having to claim the rights we are guaranteed, that we uncloak ourselves...it is in no less than a civil rights frame that we become fully visible" (369). This ruling raises questions about how much of the civil rights frame remains and how the relationship between disability culture and visibility will be shaped. Yet, however, it is still possible to claim that visibility has brought new opportunities.

I understand the importance of making those with impairments visible. When Cindy was in high school she spent several hours each day in the resource room on the first floor. The "regular" classes she attended were down the hall on the same level. She never went upstairs where college prep as well as honors and AP courses were offered. She remained invisible to the majority of her classmates, hidden behind the resource room (or romper room as her peers called it) door. Chorus was the one class where she mixed with students from the second floor. Her lyrical soprano voice won her a place with the other singers. It was a coming out, an opportunity to be seen. With this exception, however, she remained invisible. Recently, some 10 years after her graduation, I met one of her classmates, and when I mentioned that he and Cindy had graduated together, he looked completely blank. He had never seen her.

Even as I acknowledge the benefits of enhanced visibility for those with physical or mental impairments, I want to complicate this by exploring the implications of the invisible impairment. As Cindy's case illustrates, invisibility introduces the element of choice. Cindy, and those like her, can choose whether or not to reveal a condition. Invisibility enables them to avoid (temporarily, at least) the regulation that comes with visibility. As is true for any kind of passing, the choice of how to handle invisibility carries risks, but the fact remains that disability is moved out of the realm of the visible. Furthermore, invisibility demonstrates the limitations of the gaze of the teacher, showing how easy it is to misinterpret in the act of reading another's body.

Disability studies can inform our pedagogy, and it can also add valuable new perspectives to our research. Much of the current debate about educational research can be described as bound up with contests about the categories that are often assigned to those included in our investigations. That is, disagreements between those who operate within different research paradigms often focus on whether it is more appropriate to accept or interrogate categories such as "gifted," "at-risk" or "disabled." Contest also surrounds the relationship between the researcher and the subject of research. Oliver (1990) writes, the "social relations of research production…are built upon a firm distinction between the researcher and the researched" (102). Disability studies adds new dimensions to this discussion. As Simi Linton (1998) puts it, a disability studies perspective informs thinking about "issues such as autonomy, competence, wholeness, independence/dependence, physical appearance, aesthetics, community, and notions of progress and perfection" (118). Such issues frequently appear as the "variables" in our research, variables isolated from all the complexity and unclear distinctions that disability studies introduces.

Much of the research currently being done in education depends upon narrow and carefully delimited categories. The subjectivity of individuals is referenced by terms such as "at-risk" or "gifted" or "disabled." These designations assume a single and stable identity, something that the postmodern emphasis upon multiplicity and fragmentation cannot encompass. Furthermore, such monolithic designations conflate physical and political terms. Disability studies distinguishes between impairment (in hearing, vision, mobility or brain function) from disability as a way of asserting the difference between the two. As Brugemann et. al. (2001) put it, "Impairment is a physical difference…disability is what society makes of that impairment" (372-73) This occurs because of a political system that privileges some by offering them many choices, and oppresses others by limiting the options available to them. Impairment need not lead to oppression nor to a less powerful political position unless society chooses to do so. Research that employs unexamined categories like "disabled" helps to perpetuate a blurring of the physical and the political. It also makes the continuity between the impaired and the temporarily able-bodied (TAB) less visible.

Cindy has shared much of her Native American heritage with me over the years, and this experience has taught me how differently society can define the relationship between the physical and the political. The most powerful illustration of this occurred when I joined Cindy on a trip to the Yukon Territory in Canada, where her birth family lives. Her grandfather had recently died after spending several years in declining health, unable to care for himself. Her grandmother was still alive, but she, too, needed care and was living in the home of a granddaughter. When we reached our destination, Cindy and I stopped at the local Kaska band office to ask a few questions. As I walked into the lobby, I saw five large black and white photographs hanging over the receptionist's desk. I recognized two of them from pictures I'd seen earlier; one was of Cindy's grandfather, and another was of her grandmother. In response to my questions, the receptionist explained that all of these photographs were of the honored elders of the community, the people to whom members of the band council looked for advice. These frail elderly people could certainly be described as disabled—I later met Cindy's grandmother and marveled at how she managed to talk between gasping from the oxygen tank to which she was tethered. Yet they were revered as elders within the community; their physical impairment did not prevent them from having political power.

Sharing my life with Cindy has also taught me about the continuity between the impaired and the temporarily able-bodied. Cindy has difficulty retrieving names and labels. She will often say "my friend" because she can't remember a person's name, and when I cannot retrieve a word I want, I am reminded of our similarities. Categorizing and logical-sequential thinking pose challenges for Cindy; even a task as mundane as sorting socks can be hard for her, and following a series of instructions or developing a detailed plan of action independently are impossible. While these things are relatively easy for me, I have real difficulty orienting myself in space. I have no sense of direction and frequently lose my car in parking structures, unless Cindy is there to guide me. Cindy's and my complementary sets of skills remind me how easy and false labels like "disabled" can be.

Recognizing the continuity between the impaired and the temporarily able-bodied, particularly when this continuity is cast in a postmodern perspective, can lead to new ways of thinking about research. In addition to reminding us of the limitations of monolithic labels, this perspective suggests the importance of looking to multiple perspectives and including many voices in representations of those with impairments. Research based on a medical model of disability rarely includes the voice of the person with impairment. Instead, the voices of experts trained in education or medicine dominate the discourse. James Charlton, an advocate of disability studies, responds to this with a book titled *Nothing About Us Without Us.* By affirming the continuities that extend across varying abilities, researchers in education can develop positive alternatives for studying and representing the lives of those with impairments.

Autobiography has been identified as one of the ways that the perspective of those with impairment can be represented effectively. Works by writers like Nancy Mairs, Kenny Fries, and Tobin Siebers demonstrate the insight and understanding that can be gained from listening to the voices of those with impairments. My own experience of writing a double-voiced memoir with my daughter confirms the importance of adhering to the principle of "nothing about us without us." By rehearsing life events with Cindy and incorporating both our perceptions in the text, we have been able to create a much fuller portrayal of life with FAS than either of us could have done alone.

Still another perspective that disability studies brings to education centers on epistemology. Both our pedagogy and our research are shaped by the nature and grounds of what we take to be knowledge. The invisible impairment serves as a reminder of the dangers of crediting the visible with too much power. At the most fundamental level it challenges our ways of knowing.

Specifically, our tendency to give power to the visual leads us to construct discourses that depend upon equating what we can see with what is real. When we, for example, assume that the visible impairment assigns an individual to the category of the disabled, we assume a resemblance between the actual student before us with the community we define as "the disabled." In so doing we close out a variety of possibilities for that living, breathing student, and we express our adherence to the belief that visible physical markers offer a way of identifying those of a given community. According to this logic, a Lakota Sioux whom we see represented on television is a member of the same community as the Ojibwe person we meet on the street. The political limitations of this logic become immediately evident as we witness inter-tribal debates about the appropriate role of the federal government in Native American education or about establishing nuclear waste dumps on reservations. It would be naïve to assume that there is a coherent Native American community that shares common political views. Similarly, equating the physical body with a particular racial identity exposes a lack of psychological sophistication. Racial identity, as our multicultural society demonstrates so clearly, is very complicated and cannot be described adequately in terms of a one to one correlation with certain physical markers.

Susan Gabel (forthcoming) argues for seeing impairment as an aesthetic, as "an interpretation of oneself and one's place in the world constructed by one's experiences in the world," (5), and part of the evidence she offers in support of her claims is a description of two women. One, a wheelchair user, who can be described as visibly impaired, refuses to define herself as disabled; the other, a cancer patient with no external markers, who describes herself as disabled. Gabel concludes from her examination of these two cases that the way one looks does not necessarily construct one as "a disabled or not-disabled individual. Rather the disability identity or the disability aesthetic comes from one's experiences in the world and the meaning given to those experiences by the one having the experiences" (12). Although my argument moves in a slightly different direction because of its emphasis upon epistemology, it leads to a similar conclusion: Just as race cannot be assigned by what can be seen, so we cannot "know" the disabled/not-disabled identity of an individual on the basis of visual inspection.

The extent to which the myth of the gaze permeates our epistemology is made evident in Lennard Davis's (1997) explanation of the construction of normalcy. After noting that the concept of "normal" emerged in European culture in the nineteenth century at the same time that the field of statistics was developing, Davis suggests a powerful relationship between the two. First, though, he pauses to announce that nearly all the early statisticians were eugenicists. Then he explains: "Statistics is bound up with eugenics because the central insight of statistics is the idea that a population can be normed. An important consequence of the idea of the norm is that it divides the total population into standard and nonstandard subpopulations" (14). Eugenics, a field that positioned those with impairments as evolutionary defectives, was aided by the development of fingerprinting as a means of personal identification. This physical marking supports the idea, as Davis explains, that the body has an identity that corresponds with its essence. "By this logic, the person enters into an identical relationship with the body, the body forms the identity, and the identity is unchangeable and indelible as one's place on the normal curve" (15). Davis goes on to show how this knowledge of statistics contributed to the construction of persons with impairments as standing outside the desired norms. In other words, that which was available to visual inspection constituted a way of knowing how to categorize human beings, in accordance with the myth of the gaze.

Statistics, the concept of the norm, and the attendant notions about various populations continue to permeate much of the epistemology of our field. Both the postmodern perspective and principles of morality suggest the need to reconsider our ways of knowing.

Another dimension of an epistemology that equates the visible with the real is an assumption that what is not seen does not exist. The invisible impairment demonstrates the literal problems inherent in this line of thinking. Beyond this literal level, such an epistemology makes it impossible to assign power—or even existence—to the unseen or the unmarked. Educational research, with its attention to issues as diverse as intelligence, motivation, and learning, cannot function with an epistemology that counts only the visible as real.

What we need, I believe, is a more nuanced approach to the visible and its relationship to the invisible in education. Even as we acknowledge the power of what we can see, we need to grant an equal power to the invisible.

The force of the invisible, like that of the past upon the present, exerts itself in myriad and powerful ways. In pedagogy, in research, and in epistemology, then, we ignore the invisible at our own peril, especially in the postmodern world. We need to acknowledge that the gaze cannot penetrate illusion or reveal hidden truths. Failure to do this will ultimately undercut the power of the visible because, as the poet Marianne Moore put it, "The power of the visible/is the invisible."

References

Bruggeman, B. J., Feldmeier L. W., Dunn, P. A., Heifferon, B., and Cheu, J. (2001). Becoming visible: Lessons in disability." *Journal of the Conference on College Composition and Communication*, 368-98.

Charlton, J. I. (1998). *Nothing about us without us: Disability oppression and empowerment.* Berkeley: University of California Press.

Davis, L. J., Ed. (1997). *The disability studies reader*. New York: Routledge.

Foucault, M. (1975). *The birth of the clinic: An archeology of medical perception.* (AM Sheridan Smith, trans.) New York: Vintage.

Fries, K. (1997). *Body remember: A memoir.* New York: Dutton.

Gabel, S. (forthcoming) "Missing People: Writing Disabled Girls into Feminist Pedagogy." Unpublished manuscript in author's possession.

Gere, A. R. and Gere, C. M. (forthcoming). *Woman of the King Salmon.* Unpublished manuscript in author's possession.

Lacan, J. (1998). *Four fundamental concepts.* New York: Norton.

Larsen, N. (1997). *Passing.* New York: Penguin.

Linton, Si. (1998) *Claiming disability: Knowledge and identity.* New York: New York University Press.

Lyotard, J. F. (1993). *The postmodern condition: A report on knowledge.* (Geoff Bennington and Brian Massumi, trans.) Minneapolis: University of Minnesota Press.

Mairs, N. (1990). *Carnal acts.* New York: HarperCollins.

Oliver, M. (1990). *The politics of disablement: A sociological approach.* New York: St. Martin's Press.

5 Rewriting Critical Pedagogy from the Periphery: Materiality, Disability, and the Politics of Schooling

Nirmala Erevelles

Historically, disabled people have always lived at the margins of the margins of our social world, under conditions of extreme economic deprivation, political isolation, and social exclusion. This is especially true in the context of U.S. public education—a context which has continued to support discriminatory educational policies where more than five million students with disabilities experience segregation in special education programs that are, in effect, both separate and unequal (Kerzner & Gartner, 1996). In fact, disability studies scholars have struggled with the nature versus culture debate producing their own dichotomy of impairment versus disability that mirrors in many ways the feminist debates regarding sex versus gender (Corker & French, 1999; Linton 1998). For disabled scholars this differentiation brings with it its own unique problems. While, on the one hand, disabled scholars have argued that disability is, in fact, a social construction, they are, on the other hand, eager to recognize their unique phenomenological experiences of having an impairment—experiences that mark their bodies as irreducibly different from normal bodies and yet, at the same time, are integral to their identity as disabled people. It is in this context that disabled scholars find themselves caught between a rock and a hard place because while, on one level de-linking disability from impairment will expose the social construction of their oppression, at another level this de-linking will be unable to adequately account for the complexity embedded in the formation of disabled identity. However, in this essay, I am treating both *disability* and *impairment* as synonymous. In other words, I am arguing that just like disability, the meanings and the experiences associated with impairment are also historically and materially constituted and that the natural/biological is almost always historical. It is for these reasons that throughout the essay I use the term *disability* to refer to both the "disability as social construct" and "disability as impairment."

Depending on the severity of their disability, the skills learned in these segregated special education classes have permitted only a few disabled people to be employed in jobs located at the lowest rungs of the social division of labor while many more swell the ranks of the permanently unemployed, dependent on the welfare state for their daily survival. It is on account of these conditions that the World Summit on Social Development held in Copenhagen in 1995 reported that disabled people now constitute one of the largest minority groups in the world facing poverty, unemployment, and social and cultural isolation (World Summit for Social Development, 1995). In the United States itself, according to 1995 data, working people with disabilities earned only 63.6% as much, on average, as those without disabilities, resulting in nearly 30% of this working population (ages 16 to 64) living below the poverty line (LaPlante et al., 1996). Moreover, 35.8% of the people with severe disabilities who are prevented from working at all and hence qualify for Medicaid or Supplemental Security Income (SSI) have incomes below the poverty level.

Despite the material reality of these oppressive conditions experienced by disabled people, radical theorists of difference (e.g., antiracists, feminists, Marxists, queer theorists) have consistently avoided any critical discussion of the social category of disability. Often their perfunctory acknowledgments of disability reflect the add-and-stir policy that once used to haunt race, feminist, and queer theory. Such cursory gestures are generally representative of a debilitating paralysis that most critical theorists of education face when confronted by the overwhelming physiology disability has come to represent and embody. In an effort to redress these omissions in this chapter, I locate the conceptual category of disability as the central ordering force within the social relations of schooling and explore the radical possibilities that could be made available to critical pedagogies of schooling if examined from the standpoint of a materialist disability studies.

The central question I take up in this chapter is to explore how difference vis-à-vis disability is organized within schools. In other words, I am arguing in this chapter that disability plays an important role as the central analytic that organizes social difference within schools along the axes of race, class, gender, and sexual orientation. In the first section of this chapter, I critically examine the ways in which critical theory/pedagogy has addressed the issue of social difference, mapping out the limitations and possibilities of these theories when examined from the theoretical standpoint of disability studies. Then, in the second section of this chapter, I will make an argument for a materialist disability studies that I argue will not only destabilize discursive constructions of social difference, but will also challenge and reconstitute the historical, economic, political, and cultural structures that impact educational contexts.

Disability Studies Meets Critical Theory/Pedagogy

Scholars in the area of disability studies in education have been critical of the medical discourses that have historically dominated special education and that have contributed to the continued marginalization of students with disabilities in educational contexts. Arguing against the traditional notion of disability as a problem located in bodies, disability studies scholars have argued that disability is, in fact, "a problem located in the interaction between bodies and the environment in which they are situated" (R. G. Thomson, 1997, p. 296). Based on this assumption, Meekosha and Jakubowicz (1996) describe disability as "a socially constituted and reproduced set of relationships within which impairment is given social meaning and people experience processes of power directed at their bodies" (p. 79). Such definitions of disability are found to be conspicuously missing in the scholarship of prominent educational theorists whose silence on the topic can be taken as their unquestioned support of the dominant paradigm pertaining to disability.

In this section of the chapter, I will foreground both the limitations and possibilities inherent in critical theory/pedagogy of education when examined from the standpoint of disability studies. Critical of how educational theorists have regarded disability as a "minoritizing" discourse limited to a "narrow, specific, relatively fixed population or area of inquiry" (R. Thomson, 1997, p. 22), I will argue for a more "universalistic" dimension of disability studies by demonstrating its relevance not only for students with disabilities, but also nondisabled students in U.S. public schools. Influenced by the scholarship of both academics and activists who have participated in the Disability Rights Movement, I argue that for critical theory/pedagogy to be truly emancipatory, it is necessary to create theories "that conceptualize disabled and nondisabled people as integral, complementary parts of a whole universe" (Linton, 1998, p. 129). At the same time, I also argue that it is necessary to critically examine "historical and cross-cultural research on practices that divide communities along disability lines, as well as those that unite people and promote equity" (Linton, 1998, p. 129). In the early 1970s, the critical tradition in education that emerged began to examine the ways in which schools reproduced social difference along the axes of race, class, and gender. Rejecting traditional educational discourses that upheld the liberal humanist version of the rational, unified, stable, and unique subject, critical theorists of education began to propose alternative theories pertaining to the social construction of subjectivity. For example, Bowles and Gintis (1976) in *Schooling in Capitalist America* argued that the history of public education in capitalist America was a reflection of the history of the successes, failures, and contradictions of capitalism itself. In other words, they conceptualized schools as Ideological State Apparatuses, that, rather than attempting to meet the *needs* of its citizens, have instead devised administrative, curricular, and pedagogical practices that reproduce subject positions which sustain exploitative class hierarchies. For example, they argued that one way educational institutions legitimate the distribution of wealth, privilege, and status in capitalist societies is through the administration of tests that claim to measure intelligence—a presumably genetic attribute—which has then been used to support the ideology that the poor are poor because they are stupid. Consequently, schools socialize the working-class poor to accept individual responsibility for the conditions of poverty and discrimination that continue to prevent them from adequately meeting even their basic needs. In this way, schools legitimate the existence of an unequal social division of labor that locates the source of economic failure, not in the social and economic structures of capitalism, but in the individuals themselves.

Critical of this position, Bowles and Gintis, on the other hand, demonstrated through several statistical analyses that "inequality under capitalism is rooted not in individual deficiencies, but in the structure of production and property relations" (1976, p. 123). Thus, this materialist analysis that places the locus of economic success/failure in the economic structures of capitalist society rather than on the individual is similar to the arguments made by disability studies theorists. However, despite the easy application of this analysis to disability, Bowles and Gintis avoid making this critical connection. For example, even though Bowles and Gintis have argued that this frequently touted relationship between cognitive/technical ability and economic success masks the ideological interests of capitalism to justify social inequality along the axes of race, class, and gender, they shy away from applying similar analyses to the category of disability. Conversely, Bowles and Gintis actually use disability to mark the limits of their theoretical claims when they state that "the standard educational practice of using IQ and test scores as a criterion for access to higher educational levels has little merit in terms of economic (not to mention educational) rationality and efficiency, *except perhaps for the extremes of the IQ distribution curve*" (1976, p. 9; emphasis added). Clearly, the populations who are classified at the lower extreme of the IQ distribution curve are disabled people, especially those with moderate to severe/multiple disabilities. Even so, in light of their materialist explanation of how and why ability is socially constructed in capitalist societies, I find Bowles and Gintis's perfunctory dismissal of disability contradictory, to say the least. Notwithstanding these persistent oversights, I would like to argue here that Bowles and Gintis's critique of capitalist education could prove useful in extending as well as (re)writing the theoretical terrain of critical pedagogy if addressed from the standpoint of disability. In fact, I find the most persuasive aspect of their analyses to be their materialist interpretation of the concept of intelligence/ability. If we accept intelligence/ability to be historically constituted within the structures of production and property relations, then would it not be possible to offer a similar materialist analysis for the category of (dis)ability and as a result explore the implications this analysis may have on the organization of social difference in U.S. public schools? For example, if we accept Bowles and Gintis's argument that educational institutions have utilized the concept of intelligence/ability to legitimate racial, gendered, and class inequalities in both schools as well as society at large, then would this not imply that there is a relationship between the category of disability and other categories of social difference like race, class, gender, and sexuality? How, then, would a critical theory of education adapt its analyses to acknowledge this relationship and what benefits could be derived from such analyses? Further, given Bowles and Gintis's suggestion that we need to retheorize the current alienating and exploitative relationship of the working classes and labor, what would this retheorization look like from the standpoint of disability? More specifically, what arrangement of social and economic conditions would be supportive of an alternative theorization of labor such that the self-worth, needs, and desires of disabled people will not be dismissed, denigrated, or completely ignored?

Despite the emancipatory possibilities apparent in this argument, other critical theorists of education have sought to distance themselves from the economic determinism perceived in this argument, especially the subordination of cultural issues to class analyses. Conversely, critical theorists like Paul Willis (1981), Henry Giroux (1983), and Angela McRobbie (1991), influenced by the impact of poststructural theory on cultural studies, have argued that rather than being passive participants in the reproduction process, teachers and students have been active in the production of oppositional meanings and practices that constantly challenge dominant cultural practices. In making this argument, the new critical theorists of education now argue that the political economy of the sign has become "the primary category for understanding how identities are forged within particular relations of privilege, oppression, and struggle" (Giroux, 1989, pp. 121–122). This conceptual shift by critical theorists of education has produced a slew of studies that explore how the dynamics of class, race, gender, and sexuality find expression in the individual experiences, oppositional practices, and social relationships of marginal populations in educational contexts (see, e.g., Fordham, 1996; Tierney, 1997; Roman & Eyre, 1997). These studies have therefore contributed to critical education theory by recognizing those students labeled marginal/deviant as conscious agents struggling to negotiate and create an alternative oppositional intelligibility. Once again, though, notwithstanding the emancipatory possibilities that these studies promise, the voices of disabled students as oppositional subjects/agents have remained conspicuously absent in this diverse array of counter-narratives.

One of the reasons for this exclusion is that once again the category of disability is utilized by critical theorists as the boundary condition that marks the limits of human agency. For example, Kathleen Weiler points out that, "[c]entral to Giroux's discussion of ideology is his insistence that ideology also implies *the capacity for critical thinking and a transformative consciousness*" (1988, p. 23; my emphasis). Such an argument presumes a definition of human agency that persons especially with moderate to severe disabilities may find difficult to support. Disability scholar Philip Ferguson explains:

> The very epistemology of the minority group assumes that humans are agents in the social interpretation of their world, rather than as reactors to our confrontations with an unchanging world of facts that are "out there" in the "real world." The challenge of profound retardation, however, is precisely how close it seems to come to the absence of agency. It is not just that passivity is often enforced by limbs that do not move or environmental barriers that trap the individual physically. One reason for the almost total absence of qualitative research with profoundly retarded and multiply handicapped individuals is the difficulty in conceiving the social world of someone whose experience of concepts and communications is so uncertain for us. The relativity of language seems inadequate explanation. (1988, p. 54)

Clearly, based on Ferguson's observation, the social category of disability challenges any easy acceptance of difference. Thus, critical theorists of education, rather than confronting the central issue of how to (re)configure "human agency" in the face of real physiological differences, have chosen to either avoid discussion of the category alltogether or to add disability arbitrarily to the expanded sociological trinity of race, class, and gender.

It is in this context that the poststructural turn in critical theories of education with its critique of humanist constructions of subjectivity may prove to be useful. This is because poststructural theory has disrupted humanist notions of the rational, unified, and individualistic subject-agent and has replaced this with the indeterminate subject constituted and reconstituted through language in multiple, imprecise, and conflicting ways. Using this critique, Giroux has argued for similar disruptions on the pedagogical front by proposing a critical redefinition of the category of "border" as recognition of those "forms of transgression in which existing borders forged in domination can be challenged and redefined" (Giroux, 1992, p. 28). Clearly, this mode of retheorizing could disrupt the defining borders that have been historically utilized to marginalize/silence/exclude disabled students in educational settings and could therefore offer radical possibilities for critical theories of education. For example, since disabled persons with severe/multiple disabilities may be dependent on technology as well as non-disabled people to communicate, would not the disruption of the humanist version of the stable, coherent, and individualistic subject produce corresponding disruptions to traditional notions of "human agency"? As a result, what alternative/expanded definitions of "agency" would be needed in order to actually "hear" the voices of disabled students using non-traditional modes of augmentative communication? In light of such possibilities, how, then, will critical educational theory accommodate these "new" oppositional voices in its (re)theorization of difference? Further, how would such (re)theorizations of difference propose radically new ways of reorganizing classroom space, school curriculum, pedagogical practices, and classroom assessment that will be supportive of alternative/radical notions of what it means to be a "critical" human being?

However, the fact that critical theorists of education have not recognized disabled people as critical agents does not in any way imply that disabled people have passively waited around for this recognition. Conscious of their experiences of social, economic, and political subjugation, disabled scholars and activists have struggled to claim space, voice, and power to disrupt the normative ideals of the social world that has historically ignored them. To achieve this end, they have sought to define a disability culture that is based on the recognition of their *different* bodies—not in spite of their disabilities but because of them. As disabled feminist Susan Wendell explains:

> We are dis-abled. We live with particular social and physical struggles that are partly consequences of the conditions of our bodies and partly consequences of the structures and expectations of our societies, but they are struggles which only people with bodies like ours experience. (1996, p. 117)

By arguing for the recognition of disability as central to the experiences of disabled people, scholars in disability studies have shifted the locus of analysis on to the material body, and in particular the disabled body. This shift has, in fact, paralleled a similar shift in poststructural theory where the body is no longer treated as an ahistorical, pre-cultural, and/or natural object, but is instead conceived as "the site on which meanings of identity, difference, desire, knowledge, social worth, and possibility are assimilated and contested" (Kelly, 1992; p. 31). This recognition of the poststructuralist body as volatile and transgressive has therefore supported a new strand of educational theories that have begun to map the relationship between educational institutions and bodies.

Poststructural theorists of education have argued that because schools are organized such that both teachers and students are positioned into rationality, they serve to actively silence discussions that attend to the psychic and political nature of embodied knowledges, especially when these knowledges relate to a critical understanding of the workings of difference. In place of this silencing Kelly has suggested that radical pedagogies should provide the opportunities for teachers and students to explore the subjective embodiment of desire as it is mobilized in and through social forms and practices within schools. Thus, for example, some poststructuralist feminist educators have described teaching itself as an erotic, passionate, and dangerous act—the site of disturbing pleasures. The collective goal of this pedagogy is to attain *jouissance*—the pleasure derived from subverting/exploding dominant/repressive meaning systems that regulate identity formation as well as from recognizing the ambiguity, precariousness, and un-decidability of meaning-systems themselves.

This poststructural turn in critical theories of education that defines the purpose of radical pedagogy as constructing transgressive embodied knowledge and the classroom as a space of seduction, desire, authority, and resistance can actually hold amazing possibilities for the disabled student. After all, the disabled student embodies the "unruly" subject whose physiological excesses are seen to disrupt the disciplined control of schooling. In fact, the actual existence of special education programs that serve children with a variety of labels—learning disability, emotional and behavioral disorders, mild, moderate, and multiple disabilities—are predicated on the inability of regular schooling to effectively control the disruptive interruptions of these bodies that appear impervious to the rigid demands for conformity and rationality in schools. Described in these terms, the (dis)abled body can therefore be perceived as epitomizing the transgressive body of poststructural discourses. In other words, it could be argued that the disabled body, notwithstanding its marginal status, can resist the disciplining discourses of schooling by producing disruptive narratives that will "blow apart the fictions" (Kelly, 1992; p. 519) that have located it outside the scope of desire.

On exploring the transgressive possibilities of this poststructuralist position, it could be argued that the disabled subject could transform him/herself into a subject of desire by deploying subversive interventions inspired by Deleuze and Guattari's invention of the "Body-without-Organs," Butler's theory of "performativity and citationality," and Haraway's dreams of "cyborgean entities," so as to read alterity inscribed on the body in multiple and transgressive ways (see, e.g., Deleuze & Guatarri, 1983; Butler, 1993; Haraway, 1991). Here, desire is defined as both autonomous and productive in its own right such that "[desire] is not bolstered by needs, but rather the contrary; needs are derived from desire: they are counterproducts within the real that desire produces" (Deleuze & Guatarri, 1983, p. 29). Based on these claims, this poststructuralist formulation severs the relationship between desire and need, and in doing so, has (re)conceptualized consumption (desire) as *the* productive force within the social relations of capitalism, such that the social is now reconceptualized as "a scene of desire and enjoyment that is postneed, postclass, postlabor, and postproduction" (Ebert, 1996, p. 58).

However, I am going to argue here that, notwithstanding the poststructural emphasis on desire, for most disabled people, it is *need* that is foregrounded in their struggle for social justice, and not *desire*. In fact, referring to the statistics I had reported earlier, even though the disabled subject has historically occupied unruly spaces where (ir)rationality, (in)coherency, (in)completeness, and contingencies abound, these excessive embodied experiences have done little to alleviate other experiences of extreme poverty and involuntary social and economic segregation. As a result, many disabled people are compelled to be dependent on state welfare for their daily survival and are therefore relegated to the role of consumer within the social order, while at the same time not making any observable contribution to economic production. However, unlike the wealthy bourgeois consumer whose separation from the world of production is, in fact, celebrated because of his/her independent access to capital, the disabled subject's singular role as a consumer is deemed parasitic and is especially despised for his/her (non)location on the social division of labor. Therefore, in the specific historical context of capitalism, where it is individualism that is valued and not interdependence, the disabled subject is seen to inhabit a "despised body" and is relegated to the zone of Terror in the social sphere.

Materializing Disability

In this section of the chapter I am going to argue for a critical theory of education that takes into account the actual conditions of disabled people's lives. To do so, I argue that it is necessary to (re)turn to historical materialism and political economy. Arguing for this shift, I echo James Charlton's claim that "[p]olitical economy is crucial in constructing a theory of disability oppression because poverty and powerlessness are cornerstones of the dependency people with disabilities experience" (Charlton, 1998, p. 23). More importantly, political economy is concerned with not only how the everyday lives of individuals, families, and communities are incorporated into unequal social relations of power and privilege that are structured by the specific economic relations of production and consumption, it also attempts to explain why some bodies are valued more than other bodies within historically specific social relations. In fact, it is the latter question (*why disability?*) that I privilege in this discussion so as to expose the logic(s) that is/are used to maintain the exploitative conditions in which most disabled people live.

Unlike poststructuralist discourses that see the body as wholly constituted through an endless chain of significations, historical materialism reads the subject—its body, consciousness, and meanings—as produced by and through labor. This is because, as Marx and Engels have argued in the *The German Ideology*, "the first premise of all human existence and, therefore, of all history...[is] that men [sic] must be in a position to live in order to 'make history,'" (Marx & Engels, 1989, p. 48) and in order to live they need to labor. Therefore, in order to explore the question, "Why disability?" via historical materialism, I will argue here that it is important to explore where disabled people are located along the social division of labor, why it is that this location has produced conceptualizations of disability that are exclusionary and exploitative, and how such a location benefits capitalism in particular ways.

As I had discussed earlier, most disabled people, especially those with severe/multiple disabilities, have either been completely excluded from participating in economic activity or are located at the lowest rungs of the social division of labor. This is because the social category of disability (unlike other categories of difference) has been historically associated with medical conceptions of disease—a condition that has, in turn, been associated with inconvenience, nonproductivity, weakness, lack of autonomy, and incapacity. While many disabled scholars may concede that certain aspects of the disability experience may impede functioning in a world whose organization is based on particular conceptions of "normality" and may even admit that disabled people often require complex medical interventions to sustain them on a daily basis, they would nevertheless argue that it is not really their "differences" (no matter how significant they may be) that are at issue here. Rather, what is at issue is how the social world has "read" these differences. Thus, disability scholars, for the most part, have appealed to liberal constructivist theories in an effort to shift the emphasis from the disabled individual's personal "inadequacies" or functional "limitations," in order to foreground the inadequacies and/or exclusionary aspects of the social and cultural environment that is geared towards a "normal" world.

While liberal constructivist theories have focused primarily on the sociocultural sphere, I am arguing here that these theories also need to explore what impact the social relations that are constituted via capitalism have on the disabled subject. In a context where the capitalist market is governed by the laws of extraction of maximum surplus, individual citizens are required to demonstrate their capacity to be productive, efficient, and competitive participants in the workforce in order to meet the exacting demands of the market. Here I would like to draw attention to the fact that the criteria that are used to allocate people along the social division of labor are themselves historical constructions. Productivity, for example, is not an objectively established given. Instead, it is only within specific historical relations of capitalism that productivity derives its meaning via the ways in which commodified labor is linked to the generation of profits (exchange value) rather than to the satisfaction of human needs (use value). Therefore, in a context where laboring bodies are commodified and assigned differing exchange values, the disabled body with its complex (ir)regularities is seen to resist attempts to commodify it and on account of this intractability is relegated to the lowest rungs along the social division of labor and/or completely excluded from participating in the market. Alternatively, if, within another set of social relations, the laboring body is not commodified but is instead associated with the production of use-value, then in this case it would indeed be possible to explore the use-fullness of the disabled body in more creative ways, since usefull-ness is no longer predicated on generating profit but is, instead, associated with meeting perhaps some affective and/or other nonmonetary human needs.

More importantly, some disability scholars using materialist analyses have also argued that the category of disability has been utilized by capitalism to justify the exploitation and/or exclusion of certain social groups from participating in economic activity (see, e.g., Farber, 1968; Finkelstein, 1980; Nibert, 1995; Oliver, 1992). For example, they have pointed out that capitalism, in particular, needs a surplus labor market to minimize costs of production and is, therefore, required to maintain certain levels of unemployment. However, instead of describing unemployment as a necessary component of the economy, capitalist ideologies justify the exclusion of particular populations from the world of work by claiming that these individuals lack specific physical, social, and/or technical characteristics that are deemed desirable for the economy and are therefore designated as the surplus population that has historically included disabled people, the aged, as well as the permanent racialized and gendered underclass. By certifying these populations as incapable of producing for exchange value, the members of this surplus population are, in turn, certified as eligible to receive monetary aid as well as social services and are, consequently, subject to the regulatory and controlling benevolence of the welfare state (Stone, 1984). In this context then, it is possible to see how disability is used as an ideological category to justify a social division of labor along the axes of race, class, and gender.

Now, if we were to shift this analysis to the context of schooling, echoes of this argument can also be found in Bowles and Gintis's critique of capitalist schooling, where they had identified the attributes associated with the construct of intelligence/ability as reflective of the historically appropriate business values and social relationships that sustain capitalism's continued profitability. Moreover, even though Bowles and Gintis have used disability to mark the theoretical limits of their argument, I will argue here that extending their argument to address disability as a historical rather than as a natural category supports interesting analytical possibilities. For example, the everyday functioning of public schooling is predicated on the institutionalization of a complex array of evaluation strategies that are used to predict the productive capacity of future workers. Using the results of these evaluative tests, students are segregated on the basis of their "natural" abilities and labeled either "gifted," "regular," and/or "special" and assigned to different curricula that educate them for their designated slot along the social division of labor. Furthermore, Bowles and Gintis have themselves pointed out that these tests have been effective in rewarding students for their personal motivation to succeed in capitalist societies, while, at the same time, compelling students to conform to the hierarchical organization of the social order that it upholds (citizenship). However, as I had explained earlier, because disabled students have historically been perceived as unruly subjects who have consistently disrupted the ordered functioning of schooling and who have consistently resisted the disciplining forces that are called into play, they have been banished to special education classrooms to be (re)habilitated in an effort to enable them to (re)turn to normal life. In light of this scenario, it would be apt to use Thomas Skrtic's description of special education "as the profession that emerged in 20th century America to contain the failure of public education to educate its youth for full political, economic, and cultural participation in [a] democracy" (Skrtic, 1991, p. 24).

Additionally, an alternative reading of the social history of public schooling can highlight a critical relationship between disability and the other social categories of difference. Educational historians have documented that compulsory mass public education became a reality as a societal response to the turmoil of the times brought about by the Civil War; the subsequent industrialization, urbanization, and rapid economic growth that ensued; and the increasing influx of immigration to the United States. Therefore, in an effort to obscure the incompatibility between the democratic ideology of the common school and the social reality of the class structure so as to support an assimilated, integrated, and disciplined society, it became necessary to construct and disseminate ideologies that would justify the unequal social divisions of labor within the capitalist economy, especially those that were organized along race, class, and gender lines. It is in this context then, I am arguing that the category of disability became prominent in educational discourses.

For example, Sarason and Doris (1979) have pointed out that the first special education classes in the United States housed the urban poor, new immigrants, Native Americans, and African Americans. The justification of this separation of public education into regular and special education classes was based on results of psychometric tests like Alfred Binet's intelligence scales that supported a hereditary theory of IQ (Gould, 1981), and that drew relationships between mental illness, moral degeneracy, pauperism, and race, class, and gender. While these eugenic policies were no longer in vogue by the late 1960s, their influence continued in American public schools to such an extent that as late as 1968, an article by L. M. Dunn indicated that nearly 60% to 80% of pupils taught in special education classes were African American, Native American, Hispanics, non-English speakers, and children from non-middle-class backgrounds (Dunn, 1968). This occurred, despite the fact that the 1954 pivotal court case, *Brown v. Board of Education*, rendered the segregational policies of public education on the basis of race unconstitutional. In fact, this segregation was justified by drawing on the logic of disability to claim that these students were unable to meet the normative standards of the regular classroom. Thus, despite the legal mandate for desegregation, American public education has used the category of disability to support separate regular education and special education programs that assign students oppressively marked by race, class, and gender to lower tracks within the educational matrix that correspond to similar tracks within the larger social and economic order.

In light of the situation I have just alluded to, it is indeed ironic that the 1975 Education for All Handicapped Children Act (PL 94–142) was modeled after *Brown v. Board of Education*, where students with disabilities were now, by legal mandate, to be integrated into classrooms that represented the least restrictive environment. In fact, within some education circles, the passing of PL 94–142 was interpreted as a progressive move that was going to address the last bastion of inequality in U.S. public education in an effort to respond effectively to the moral imperative of equal opportunity for all citizens. However, by the late 1970s, much of this optimism was tempered by new educational policy decisions that came in the wake of the perception that the U.S. economy was appearing to lose its hegemonic control of the global economy. It was in this context that another landmark education policy document, *A Nation at Risk*, was circulated in 1983 that supported new education policies which more emphasis on issues of excellence as opposed to equity—with detrimental effects for students who benefited from the compensatory/inclusive programs in previous years.

Therefore, in recent years, despite the move to integrate more students with disabilities into regular classrooms, new labels, like "at risk," "learning disabled," "emotionally handicapped," "gifted and talented" have emerged in order to continue to segregate children in the name of increasing standards so as to maintain a competitive edge in global markets as well as to ensure that the capitalist class in the United States maintains global economic dominance. Interestingly enough, the bulk of these special classes continue to be populated by students who have been marked in oppressive ways by race, class, and/or gender. For example, both Christine Sleeter (1987) and Barry Franklin (1987) have drawn linkages between the construction of the categories of learning disability and emotional disturbance and the continued maintenance of race, class, and gender divisions in society. In this way, we can see how special education through the articulation of an ideology of disability appeals to abstract notions of efficiency, rationality, and equity rooted in a seemingly open, objective, and meritocratic science in order to reproduce in abstract form the dominant class relationships, divisions of labor, and cultural hegemony present in twentieth- and twenty-first century America.

It could be argued that by emphasizing economic issues, I may ignore the possibilities that exist within alternative counter-ideological spaces of resistance. Taking this aspect into consideration, it could be argued that the reforms that took place after PL 94–142 mandated the integration of students with disabilities in regular classrooms, have actively challenged dominant discursive constructions of disability by utilizing pedagogical practices like individualizing curricula, utilizing cooperative learning groups, and reworking assessment procedures so as to highlight the potential of even the most severely disabled students. By radically exploring the potential of disabled individuals in creative ways, these practices have also played a major part in redefining concepts of disabled and normal and have therefore done extensive work in constantly redrawing the borders of special and regular education. Thus, it could be argued that the integration of students with disabilities into regular classrooms could be perceived as one example of a border pedagogy that acts so as to re-inscribe the terrain of difference in new and radical ways.

However, even though I may celebrate these resistant practices, I cannot afford to ignore the critical reality that schools are increasingly located right at the heart of the social division of labor that marks distinctions between mental and manual labor. As a result of this division, Apple describes how schools and universities continue to appropriate a curriculum that differentiates between "those whose later surplus labor can be utilized for the construction of new technological/administrative knowledge and [therefore] located within the slots of mental labor," whereas there are others like students of difference "who rejected by this particular calculus of values are 'placed' through internal guidance and curricular programs in a trajectory that allows surplus labor to be later extracted from them in the form of service and/or manual labor" (Apple, 1995, p. 46). Therefore, despite the ways in which proponents of inclusive education have worked toward radically redefining the field of education, these redefinitions still exist within a social and economic context that nevertheless demand productivity and efficiency as the hallmarks of success within capitalism—concepts that have historically required the category of disability to enable schools to perform such sorting practices effectively. This supports Ebert's other claim that

> [c]lass societies naturalize the social division of labor by means of pre-given ("natural") attributes such as sex, race, age, gender. Difference in class societies is the difference of economic access, which is determined by the position of the subject in the social relations of production. Difference, in other words, is socially produced at the site of production. However, it is secured and legitimated by reference to the natural features of the workers (age, race, gender) in order to keep down the cost of labor power (the only source of value) and thus increase the level of profit. (1996, p. 91)

Following from the logic of Ebert's argument, I would like to advance my own. I will argue here that from the above discussion, it appears that disability, or what has been otherwise commonly understood as deviant difference, has been historically used to justify and to regulate the ways by which the accumulation of surplus is allocated to a small yet powerful minority belonging to the capitalist class. Moreover, examining this hypothesis within the broader context of global political economy, it is possible to see how the ideology of disability has been used to justify, first the sexual division of labor which constructed gender as a political and economic concept, the production of class/caste differences that first sustained the feudal order and later capitalism, the production of racial categories generated by the imperialistic practices of slavery, colonialism, and now neo-colonialism; and the upholding of compulsory heterosexuality so as to preserve "family values" in an effort to naturalize the oppressive systems that allow for capitalist accumulation to take place. Using the above logic, I have therefore tried to show how disability has been used by U.S. public education as the underlying ideology to legitimate who gets what allocations, even in the face of claims to a liberal democracy.

Increasingly, on account of the economic crisis in the United States and the shifting of production processes to off-shore locations with its concomitant effects of rising unemployment, it is becoming frighteningly evident that public schools and the associated "special" services they provide may soon outlive their usefulness to the economy. Whereas before, schools also served to construct an industrial reserve army from which society could draw upon in its hour of need, the current economic changes are transforming increasing numbers of workers into a redundant population on account of the global reorganization of the social relations of production. More often than not, this group of workers, now rendered redundant, comprise the very poor—many of them being women and children coming from communities of color and/or marked by other forms of difference like disability. In the face of increased cuts in social spending and the move to privatize public schooling this abandoned population struggling at the borders are left with few resources for survival. Living under conditions that actually deny their very humanity, their only recourse is in the construction of countercultural practices that serve to disrupt the smooth workings of dominant structures. However, these ruptures in the dominant cultural practices are precisely that—ruptures—and not transformative practices—because they do very little to transform the exploitative conditions under which the working class (despite its diverse access to multiple subjectivities) has to nevertheless labor under. As a result, border pedagogies need to do much more than celebrate the transgressive possibilities that the postmodern moment has to offer.

Utopia at the Borders

In *Schooling in Capitalist America*, Bowles and Gintis argued that education policies in the early 1920s supported what they termed were "poor-as-dumb theories of inequality" (Bowles & Gintis, 1976) that were based on eugenic beliefs in racial superiority. While public education has done much to move away from its oppressive identification with such beliefs of the past, the underlying logic (i.e., the logic of disability) has not undergone any drastic transformation, but is, in fact, reinforced in more insidious ways. Thus, for example, David Nibert has pointed out that in light of the current crisis of late capitalism, where the decrease in unskilled jobs has served to reinforce the fact that there is an increasing need to be "smart" to succeed, these ideologies have been useful in constructing the conditions whereby poor, able-bodied individuals seek to distance themselves from disability by taking cold comfort in the assertion, "[We] may be poor (or black/female/queer) but [we're] not stupid" (Nibert, 1995, p. 76). Critical of these ideologies, in this essay I have therefore attempted to remove disability from its peripheral status in the analyses of difference and have instead offered a retheorization of it as the organizing/grounding principle in the construction of the categories of gender, race, and class within the context of schooling. Although I have emphasized notions of totality in an attempt to foreground the exploitative logic of the capitalist market place, this analysis does not preclude the possibility for emancipatory praxis. Such praxis, I have argued, can only be possible if we view human suffering and the dynamics of human struggle as something produced out of the economic, social, and political inter-relationality of complex structures maintained on a global scale by transnational capitalism. As a result, my proposal for an alternative form of critical pedagogy is deceptively simple. I will argue for a critical pedagogy that provides the intellectual tools that can render visible the material structures and ideological discourses that have different effects on say, black, white, lesbian, working-class, disabled, and third world students, and yet at the same time have to be transformed so that all students can achieve the social, economic, and political liberation.

References

Apple, M. (1995). *Education and power*. (2nd ed.). New York: Routledge.

Bowles, S., & Gintis, H. (1976). *Schooling in capitalist America: Educational reform and the contradictions of economic life*. New York: Basic Books.

Butler, J. (1993). *Bodies that matter: On the discursive limits of "sex."* New York: Routledge.

Charlton, J. (1998). *Nothing about us without us: Disability oppression and empowerment.* Berkeley: University of California Press.

Corker, M. & French, S. (1999). *Disability Discourse.* London: Open University Press.

Deleuze, G., & Guatarri, F. (1983). *Anti-Oedipus: Capitalism and schizophrenia.* Minneapolis: University of Minnesota Press.

Dunn, L. M. (1968). Special education for the mildly retarded—Is much of it justifiable? *Exceptional Children, 35*(1), 5–22.

Ebert, T. L. (1996). *Ludic feminism and after: Postmodernism, desire, and labor in late capitalism.* Ann Arbor: University of Michigan Press.

Farber, B. (1968). *Mental retardation: Its social context and social consequences.* Boston: Houghton and Mifflin.

Ferguson, P. (1988, summer). The social construction of mental retardation. *Social Policy,* 54.

Finkelstein, V. (1980). *Attitudes and disabled people: Issues for discussion.* New York: World Rehabilitation Fund.

Fordham, S. (1996). *Blacked out: Dilemma of race, identity, and success at Capital High.* Chicago: University of Chicago Press.

Franklin, B. (1987). The first crusade for learning disabilities: The movement for the education of backward children. In T. Popkewitz (Ed.), *The formation of school subjects: The struggle for creating an American institution.* New York: Falmer.

Giroux, H. A. (1983). *Theory and resistance in education: A pedagogy for the opposition.* South Hadley, MA: Bergin & Garvey.

——— (1989). Schooling as a form of cultural politics: Towards a pedagogy of and for difference. In H. Giroux & P. McLaren (Eds.), *Critical pedagogy, the state, and cultural struggle* (pp. 125–151). Albany: State University of New York Press.

——— (1992). *Border crossings: Cultural workers and the politics of education.* New York: Routledge.

Gould, S. J. (1981). *The mismeasure of man.* New York: Norton.

Haraway, D. (1991). *Simians, cyborgs, and women: The reinvention of nature.* New York: Routledge.

Kelly, U. (1992). *Schooling desire: Literacy, cultural politics, and pedagogy.* New York: Routledge.

Kerzner Lipsky, D., & Gartner, A. (1996). Equity requires inclusion: The future for all students with disabilities. In C. Christensen & F. Rizvi (Eds.), *Disability and the dilemmas of education and justice.* Philadelphia: Open University Press.

LaPlante, M. P., Kennedy, J., Kaye, H. S., & Wenger, B. L. (1996). *Disability and Employment: Disability Statistics.* Abstract 11. Washington, DC: U.S. Department of Education and National Institute of Disability and Rehabilitation Research.

Linton, S. (1998). *Claiming disability: Knowledge and identity.* New York: New York University Press.

Marx, K., & Engels, F. (1989). *The German ideology.* New York: International Publishers.

McRobbie, A. (1991). *Feminism and youth culture: From 'Jackie' to 'just seventeen.'* Basingstoke, Hampshire: Macmillan.

Meekosha, H., & Jakubowicz, A. (1996). Disability, participation, representation, and social justice. In C. Christensen & F. Rizvi (Eds.), *Disability and the dilemmas of education and justice.* Philadelphia: Open University Press.

Nibert, D. (1995). The political economy of developmental disability. *Critical Sociology, 21*(1), 59–80.

Oliver, M. (1992). *The politics of disablement: A sociological approach.* New York: St. Martin's Press.

Roman, L. G., & Eyre, L. (Eds.) (1997). *Dangerous territories: Struggles for difference and equality in education.* New York: Routledge.

Sarason, S., & Doris, J. (1979). *Educational handicap, public policy, and social history: A broadened perspective on mental retardation.* New York: The Free Press.

Skrtic, T. (1991). *Behind special education: A critical analysis of professional culture and school organization.* Denver, CO: Love Publishing House.

Sleeter, C. (1987). Why is there a learning disability: A critical analysis of the birth of the field in its social context. In T. Popkewitz (Ed.), *The formation of school subjects: The struggle for creating an American institution.* New York: Falmer Press.

Stone, D. (1984). *The disabled state.* Philadelphia: Temple University Press.

Thomson, R. (1997). *Extraordinary bodies.* New York: Columbia University Press.

Thomson, R. G. (1997). Integrating disability studies into the existing curriculum: The example of "women and literature" at Howard University. In L. J. Davis (Ed.), *The disability studies reader,* pp. 275-306. New York: Routledge.

Tierney, W. (1997). *Academic outlaws: Queer theory and cultural studies in the academy.* Thousand Oaks, CA: Sage.

Weiler, K. (1988). *Women teaching for change: Gender, class, and power.* New York: Bergin & Garvey.

Wendell, S. (1988). *Women teaching for change: Gender, class, and power.* New York: Bergin & Garvey.

Willis, P. (1981). *Learning to labor: How working class kids get working class jobs.* New York: Columbia University Press.

World Summit for Social Development. (1995). *Copenhagen declaration on social development, 15-h.* http://www.webonly.com/socdev/wssdco-2.htm.

6 Compliance as Alienated Labor: A Critical Analysis of Public School Programs for Students Considered to have Emotional/Behavioral Disorders

Scot Danforth

The Curriculum of Control as a Demoralizing Program

In a comprehensive national study of public school programs for students considered to have emotional-behavioral disorders (E/BD), Knitzer, Steinberg, and Fleisch (1990) visited special classrooms and schools around the United States. In their national tour, they specifically asked local school districts to allow them to visit the best and most successful programs. What they found were segregated classrooms and schools that had primarily replaced the common educational curriculum comprised of academic subject matter and learning activities with a disciplinary curriculum teaching students compliance with authority. More specifically, they located the phenomenon they called the "curriculum of control" in the systems of behavior management used by the teachers seeking obedience from the students. Typically, these systems consisted of a levels system (Bauer & Shea, 1988; Bauer, Shea, & Keppler, 1986; Smith & Farrell, 1993), a classroom microeconomy based on Skinnerian principles of positive reinforcement whereby students earn points for exhibiting specific behaviors. Points were tallied and used as capital to exchange for higher status, greater freedom, and a variety of toys, foodstuffs, and trinkets.

Though scripted in the tight and restrained language of social science, the Knitzer, Steinberg, and Fleisch (1990) study reads almost like a journalistic exposé in the tradition of Burton Blatt's (Blatt & Kaplan, 1966; Blatt, 1970) groundbreaking work on the back wards of institutions. Knitzer and her colleagues seemed to strain at the bit, perhaps wanting to sound a clarion cry for dramatic change in the systems of special education and child mental health. One could argue that the field of child mental health has responded to the crisis identified by Knitzer et al. through the intense, ongoing development of cooperative alliances between community service agencies and public schools (Stroul, Lourie, Goldman, & Katz-Leavy, 1992; Stroul, 1996). However, there is little or no indication in the special education research literature or in the realm of public school E/BD programming that the field of special education has responded in any significant way to the "curriculum of control" critique. By all accounts, the curriculum of control is alive and well.

One reason for this nonresponse may be because the Knitzer et al. "curriculum of control" critique was conceptually insufficient. It fell short of peering directly into the control regime of the segregated E/BD programs to ask what is happening and how this is affecting the lives of students. The critique failed to provide a compelling and theoretically sound analysis of what the classroom microeconomy utilized in the segregated E/BD programs means within the lives and learning of students in segregated E/BD programs. Undoubtedly, as Knitzer and her colleagues have pointed out, these E/BD programs lack a well-constructed, complete, and thoughtful academic curriculum. Students educated in a curriculum of control are taught obedience rather than school knowledge as contained in the traditional academic disciplines or practical knowledge as embodied in vocational preparation programs. Even so, to go a step further, what does it mean to the humanity of these students to be schooled in programs that offer symbolic and concrete rewards for their compliant behaviors? What does this mean in terms of the development of humans as moral and social beings?

In this essay, in a provisional and initial effort to address these issues, I turn to the humanism of Marx, specifically to his ethical theory and economic theory, to present a critique of the common levels system of behavior management used in E/BD programs. Drawing from the work of Marx (1964; 1990), Marxist theorists (Berlin, 1963; Gramsci, 1992; Fromm, 1961; West, 1991), and Marxist sociologists (Axelos & Bruzina, 1976; Erickson, 1986; Israel, 1971; Meszaros, 1970), I will elucidate the levels system of behavior management as a classroom microeconomy that translates compliant student behaviors into commodities, valuing obedience as economic objects to be traded for status and privileges. While the work of students in most public schools would be characterized as "academic" or "knowledge" work, the labor of students schooled under the curriculum of control is the production of behaviors that "earn points" and are therefore commodified into economic units of exchange. Instead of learning that human action has moral value that may be evaluated and appreciated as an expression and enactment of an agentic self, instead of learning that human action has social value that may be understood in terms of how it contributes to the lives of others, these students are systematically taught that their actions have purely economic value devoid of moral or social substance. In this sense, they are literally demoralized. Denuded of moral or social value, the students' point-earning actions are alienated labor, work that operates not to constitute and enhance the development of self in a social context but to vacate and diminish the self as moral agent in the world. This essay explains the Marxist concept of alienated labor and demonstrates how the curriculum of control creates the social conditions of alienation, an existential loss of the opportunity to constitute a thinking, acting, moral self.

Inside the E/BD Program

For anyone who has not been a student or teacher in an E/BD program— specifically, a school or residential center for students labeled E/BD—the feel and texture of such a social environment is difficult to imagine. I worked as a teacher for seven years in two residential schools and two "day" schools for students considered E/BD. I have visited and consulted with countless others over the past two decades. Although there is some degree of variability across settings, they tend to be strikingly similar. The best description of the social climate of these programs is provided by sociologist Erving Goffman (1961) in his book *Asylums*. Although Goffman's work primarily investigates the nature of institutional settings where people live, work, and play, I find his description of the basic features of "total institutions" to greatly ring true for both day schools and residential programs. Goffman (1961, p. 6) outlined four basic characteristics of "total institutions." He did not claim that all institutions have all characteristics but that these four features provide a general understanding of what tends to be common in such social settings.

(1) "(A)ll aspects of life are conducted in the same place and under the same single authority."
(2) "(E)ach phase of the member's (student's) daily activity is carried on in the immediate company of a large batch of others, all of whom are treated alike and required to do the same thing together."
(3) "(A)ll phases of the day's activities are tightly scheduled, with one activity leading at a prearranged time into the next, the whole sequence of activities being imposed from above by a system of explicit formal rulings and a body of officials."
(4) "(T)he various enforced activities are brought together into a single rational plan purportedly designed to fulfill the aims of the institution."

In the segregated class or school for students labeled E/BD, the single authority is "the school" or "the program." The "body of officials"—teachers, teachers' aides, counselors, and administrators—constitute the enacting forces of the school or program, the active embodiments of the single authority. Under that authority, the activities of all students are planned, orchestrated, monitored, and regulated. Social conformity through compliance with authority is the explicit "aim of the institution." Generally, this aim is supplemented by a more humanitarian ethos of helping troubled kids improve their behavior so that they can return to general classrooms and schools.

My general purpose in this chapter is to pry apart the political economy of this institutional model of public schooling, opening up the "single rational plan" called a levels system to critique and demystification. My conceptual vehicle in this task is Marx's theory of human labor.

Marx on Alienated Labor

> If the product of labor is alien to me, if it confronts me as an alien power, to whom then does it belong? If my own activity does not belong to me, if it is an alien, a coerced activity, to whom then does it belong? To a being other than myself. (Marx, 1964, p. 115)

Understanding the meaning of labor in Marxist thought requires that we begin with his articulation of the dehumanizing human state of alienated or estranged labor. A more fulfilling form of labor that expresses individuality as it constitutes the individual, that enacts and enriches the universality of humanity in the social realm, is best understood through first examining the opposite condition. Marx articulates the concept of estranged or alienated labor as he criticizes the social reality evident before his mid-nineteenth-century eyes. He builds a powerful critique from the moral vacuum of domination surrounding him in the early industrial world while keeping his sights set on the emancipation of truly productive, fulfilling labor. Marx's primary theme throughout this critique that occurs across multiple works over his life is the way that the social relations of production, the economic system and social organization of human labor, makes relations between human beings appear as relations between things (West, 1991, p. 44). Human living that is inherently social and shared is spun deceptively into an economic algebra of objects, things, and money reigning over humans and humanity.

Alienated or estranged labor is potentially a productive human activity the value and meaning of which is stolen from the worker by the capitalist, by the business owner who pays the worker hourly or piece rate wages for his labor. This critique pivots on the difference between what Marx (1990) calls exchange value and use value. The intrinsic, subjectively experienced meaning and value of an individual's activities is the use value, what the actual process and product of labor is qualitatively and quantitatively worth to the worker within the worker's thoughts and emotions. To be human, to Marx, is to take intentional action upon the natural and social world in an effort to alter the environment. At the most primitive level, this occurs in an effort to carve out a physical subsistence in the sense of food, clothing, and shelter. In civilized society, this human mental and physical activity goes far beyond survival goals, reaching ends of individual and cultural cultivation; the production of the objects, practices, forms, and symbols through which humans create/discover fulfillment and meaning.

Additionally, and simultaneously, the notion of use value includes not only the individual's experience of her own productive activities but also the value and meaning of that labor process and product to the community; the shared moral, aesthetic, and practical appraisal of that human effort. Marx does not split the individual life of meaning from the communal life of culture, but sees the wide range of human thought and action called labor as the constitutive expression and crafting of both in unison. Marx is not unlike John Dewey in his emphasis on the development of the individual's talents and capacities not in opposition to the furtherance of society but within the moral scope of that cultural development.

We should note that Marx's concept of use value involves the experienced utility and moral substance of human activity absent of or prior to the pervasive infiltration of the market economy. It is a concept of human value, of subjective and intersubjective worth, rather than commodified value. It is what we might call a democratic ideal but what Marx considered the natural state of humanity, a state distorted by the overlay and penetration of the capitalist relations of production. As we might quip, money ruins everything. In a capitalist market economy, labor is stripped of use value and assigned an exchange value as human labor and the products of labor are rendered into commodities for sale. Labor is granted economic value when it is traded for money, when the laborer's time and effort are exchanged for wages. Human activity is emptied of social and moral value as labor becomes the virtual equivalent to wages, as labor becomes not human action generating and enacting moral value for self and community but human motion traded coldly for wages. Human mental, physical, and social effort therefore carries a monetary value that is determined by the marketplace, effectively turning labor and money into moral and social equivalents. Labor loses use value as exchange value dominates. The subjective and communal meaning of human activity is evacuated as the worker's ownership over his own labor and the meaning of that labor is lost. Human activity is no longer human as the monetary meaning of work supercedes and dominates. The laborer trades mere motion for wages, and the laborer's time and productive behavior become objects owned by the employer.

Marx on Free and Constructive Labor

For Marx, free and constructive labor is the way that we humans make ourselves, own ourselves, create our unique identities, and define the cultural and subjective dimensions of our lives. Through our labor, embodied in a labor process and objectified in the products of labor, we simultaneously craft both the unique expression and cultivation of individuality and the complexity and unity of society. In the activities and products of human labor, the unified means and ends, individuals and societies continuously become. Labor is the variety of human mental and physical activities through which humans confront, alter, and contend with nature. However, labor extends far beyond meeting essential physical needs. It extends into the multiple realms of what we would call cultural development; the daily generation and modification of the organizations, institutions, and practices of a given way of life. All the objects, experiences, and social processes that an individual can point to and call her life, and all the associated activities that a community or society can point to as a shared way of life, are the activities and products of labor. Acting upon the world, purposefully bringing mind and body and self to the task, we humans make our lives, make our world.

Identity on the individual and collective level—the self, the community, society—is simultaneously made by that world that humans make. Through the interaction with the social and physical environment, the human acts upon external nature and changes it, and in this way he simultaneously changes his own nature (Marx, 1990, p. 283). As the hands, minds, and hearts of humans create objects and social processes of instrumental, aesthetic, productive, and cultural value, the work itself is the crucible of development for the individual. Through labor, we not only create products that express and objectify who we are. We also build our many mental and physical capacities, acquiring and maturing the practical, intellectual, and affective skills that make each individual unique and complete. Marx also views labor as the human activity through which a person creates and enacts what we would call moral character; the depth and range of intention, empathy, awareness, and action that makes up the moral dimensions of the individual. To be moral, in Marxist theory, is to live and act in awareness of one's existential relations to oneself, to other persons, and to life itself. Knowing that one is creating history B contributing to the concrete, ongoing development of the human story—in one's labor and accepting responsibility for one's interactions with nature and community members are the cornerstones of moral living. The key theme here is ownership of one's actions, of one's labor, and ownership of one's undeniable connection to humanity and community. Labor is the activity in which one finds oneself, and it is also the active means for the furtherance of the universal social bond, the inherent common humanity of all. In labor, we find the human activity that both brings about the fullest development of the individual and secures and fosters the common life, the community of shared association and meaning. Moral living, in this sense, is activity directed toward the development and fulfillment of both the individual personality and the common bond. The self and the common life are unified, harmonized, cultivated, in the labor that extends, expresses, and fulfills the self as social being.

Morality, in this light, is not so much an issue of individual choice but a question of the way that human activity is organized and structured. It is a question of whether labor is allowed to fulfill the existential and communal roles of humanity or if it is squandered, stifled, distorted, and twisted back upon itself. Is labor, human productive activity, organized in ways that foster freedom, individual development, and the cultivation of social bonds? Alternatively, is labor turned into a process that confuses social bonds with things, replaces the importance of humanity with the value of objects, devalues the laborer through an economic system that places value in money and property rather than people? That is Marx's humanistic challenge.

Level Systems: Compliant Behavior as Economic Commodity

A level system is a formalized token economy. In a token economy, students are given chips or tokens as rewards for exhibiting the specific behaviors considered desirable by the professional staff. The tokens are typically traded by the students for special privileges and snacks. The stated purpose of the level system within the professional discourse is to reduce the frequency of undesired behaviors and increase the frequency of desired behaviors (e.g., Bauer & Shea, 1988; Bauer, Shea, & Keppler, 1986; Scheuermann, 1994; Smith & Farrell, 1993). Because the definition of desired and undesired behavior resides with the school professionals, it is obvious that the system seeks student compliance with authority.

The level system as typically utilized in public school E/BD programs replaces tokens with points. Individual students are accorded points at fixed time intervals based on the exhibition of the set of desired behaviors. Point totals are generally tallied at the end of the day. The points have economic value in two specific ways. First, students use them to purchase privileges like snacks and time playing computer games. Additionally, the daily point tallies are currency for the procurement of status on a hierarchy of levels. Students on the highest status levels are given extra freedoms, fun activities, and privileges. In contrast, the activities of students on the lowest levels are tightly restricted. Often the attainment of higher levels of status requires many weeks of compliance and point-earning. Within Marx's economics, a commodity is a thing that is bought and sold through a market of economic exchange. Even a human activity becomes a thing, an object, when use value is supplanted by exchange value, when the economic worth displaces the moral and social worth. Because human activity is not naturally an object, in order for it to be exchanged on a market, it must be translated into a symbolic or objective form. It must be distilled from moral and social activity into an impersonal thing, something inhuman that can be counted, valued, and traded in monetary exchange terms. That objectified human action becomes a commodity when it is defined in terms of economic value on a marketplace of trade. The value of a commodity is created on the basis of economic exchange, a trade of that commodity for another commodity or for currency that symbolizes commodities.

Classroom level systems that compensate students with points for displaying specific behaviors effectively turn desired or compliant student behaviors into commodities. Action is translated into economic units. A given behavior attains social worth within that classroom on the basis of the exchange value of that behavior in the microeconomic system. According to the level system, an action in and of itself has no social value or moral weight until it is observed, tallied, and rewarded by an authority figure managing the system. Actions such as reading a book or kindly helping a peer are made meritorious when they are translated into economic units that are later traded for privileges, goods, or the status of the higher levels. In a total program of points that operates during every moment of the school day and bus ride, a student's every observable action may be translated into units of economic value.

Are the Educational Workers Alienated?

Alienation, first used to describe the dehumanizing experience of industrial workers, has been broadly appropriated by educational researchers to describe the way many students feel "turned off" or emotionally diminished by the experience of public education (Docking, 1990; Hickerson, 1966; Kelakin-Fishman, 1996; LeCompte & Dworkin, 1991; Leight, 1974; Liazos,

1978; Loken, 1973). Educational researchers, adopting the concept of alienation from the early writings of Marxist sociologists, have linked student
alienation with high dropout rates (Calabrese & Poe, 1991; Williams, 1987),
cheating (Calabrese & Cochran, 1990), and behavior problems (Zeeman,
1982).

However, the situation of the student schooled within the E/BD level
system is unique even within public schools that often seem dull and empty
of meaning. The level system cultivates an alienated labor of a type and degree rarely experienced by general education students. While the use of
standard systems of testing, scoring, and grading within public schools is
likely to commodify student academic labor to some degree, there is no parallel to the experience of the E/BD labeled student who receives monetary
wages for specific acts of obedience and compliance. There is no other student in the public school whose actions within the moral and social landscape of the school are automatically commodified. There is no other student
whose very educational program consists, in the eyes of the administrators
and teachers who run the level system as part of program designed to benefit the student's psychosocial development, of the demoralizing commodification of action.

The commodification of human labor in the form of compliant activity
through the level system arranges the social conditions of alienation by sub-
stituting exchange value for use value, monetary value for the moral dimensions of human labor. The specific ramifications and effects of this situation
vary greatly from school to school, class to class, and student to student.
Even so, the general conditions of alienated labor as clearly structured and
imposed by the level system must be viewed as far-reaching and powerful.
However, what are those far-reaching results? What does this alienation look
like? How does this alienation impact the life of a student? Although a body
of ethnographic research has been amassed about student alienation and resistance in general education classrooms (e.g., Foley, 1990; Giroux, 1983;
McLaren, 1985, 1993; Willis, 1977), there is no descriptive research literature
about students considered E/BD who are schooled under level systems. The
dearth of qualitative research concerning the education of students labeled
E/BD, while held to be unproblematic in most quarters of special education,
leaves us empty-handed as we ask searching questions about social experience and moral meaning.

The E/BD research literature that does exist tends to subsume the dimensions of human alienation under the contours of educational psychopathology, casting student actions of resistance, opposition, and even human
suffering beneath a general notion of individualized deficit. Basically, if the

student called E/BD is miserable and misbehaving, that is just the underlying emotional/behavioral disorder exhibiting itself. The student who does not buy into the level system, earn the rewards, work his way up the levels, and clean up his behavior is failing to overcome or cope with his disorder. His actions are assumed not to be evidence of the dulling, demoralizing effects of an alienating environment that turns obedience into wages, that turns action in the social world into commodities for market exchange. His resistance and opposition are assumed to be evidence of the disorder that landed him in the program in the first place. Moreover that disorder must be very severe if it fails to respond to the treatment called the level system.

This circular, scapegoating logic, however, does not remove our responsibility to take the alienation of students considered E/BD seriously. In the final pages of this essay, I'll draw from my own experiences teaching within E/BD level system programs in Virginia, North Carolina, and Florida to describe the multiple faces or dimensions of student alienation. I'll borrow Seeman's (1959, 1975, 1979, 1983) five-part, sociological explication of alienation as human experience as an insightful tool for understanding the experiences of students within these programs.

Five Dimensions of Alienation

Applying Marx's concept of alienated labor broadly to the many human experiences lacking subjective moral substance, Seeman (1959, 1975, 1979, 1983) provided the seminal sociological definition of alienation. He delineated the experience of alienation as occurring along five specific dimensions: powerlessness, meaninglessness, normlessness, isolation, and self-estrangement. The experience of alienation involves one or more of these five modes.

Powerlessness

Seeman (1959) describes powerlessness as "the expectancy or probability held by the individual that his own behavior cannot determine the occurrence of outcomes" (p. 784). Effort is held to be worthless given the slim chance of bringing about a positive or desired outcome. The twin pivotal themes of powerlessness are location and control; the location of the decision regarding success or failure and the degree of control over that decision held by the individual. A powerless person experiences the decision process concerning the value of her efforts as external (outside herself) and beyond her meaningful involvement or participation. Powerlessness exists when the individual feels dominated by external forces, when the positive outcomes or rewards sought are experienced as existing primarily or completely outside that individual's sphere of control.

In my experience teaching within level systems, it was very typical that students simply gave up, stopped trying to earn the points and climb the levels. Ironically, this often occurred among students who were highly successful (highly compliant) within the system. We teachers generally believed that students who were adequately reinforced for doing well (complying with authority) would enjoy the success of earning points. This success would breed a new attitude filled with self-esteem, optimism, and confidence. More often, though, we found that even these successful students quickly lost interest in the reward system.

Unfortunately, we teachers did not question the system we lived in and espoused. We failed to understand that one does not become more powerful and confident by becoming more compliant to an authority that dictates the exchange value of one's labor. We failed to ask the central question —Who decides what is good? Who decides what is valuable action? As long as this decision resides completely or primarily in the hands of authority, as long as this decision does not involve the student's meaningful participation, then the student experiences powerlessness.

Meaninglessness

Meaninglessness is based on Karl Mannheim's (1940; also see Marcuse, 1964) description of modern society as dominated by a functional rationality in which a cold mathematical efficiency replaces individual and communal ways of ordering and making sense of life events. Moral, communal, and spiritual ways of making meaning are eclipsed by impersonal, hyper-rationalized frameworks imposed by bureaucratic organizations and the capitalist marketplace. The personal salience and import of events is siphoned away as the individual loses the opportunity to intelligibly interpret and regulate her or his life and world. The individual loses the ability to construct a subjectively sensible explanation of a world that seems to be chaotic, cold, and out of reach. The key to this variation of alienation is the way that alienating circumstances bring an individual to fully doubt her or his ways of making sense of lived experience. The individual feels a lack of personal agency in constructing and experiencing meaning within and through her labor, her thoughts, feelings, and actions.

For the students called E/BD, there are two primary avenues for seeking and constructing subjective meaning. A student may take the road of compliance. He may overidentify with the system of authority, taking that economic system as a substitute for his more personal and communal forms of meaning. This requires that he sacrifice himself in an act of submission to the higher power. Such an act of identification and self-mystification reduces the student to the role of an instrumental cog within the wheels and sprockets that spin against him. He becomes a co-conspirator in his own moral evacuation. In another scenario, the student may find meaning in opposing that system, subverting it, manipulating it, pounding his fists and heart against it, turning it upside-down and inside-out. One can find intense meaning in defiance, in building an oppositional identity that narrowly stands for something only inasmuch as it stands against what is large, dominant, and blocks out the sun. Such an oppositional identity may become the focal point of fraternity and connection among the students, a brotherhood united by transgression and bonded by their disruptive quest for freedom and authentic meaning.

Normlessness

Normlessness is a situation in which the decline of community and collective standards of conduct is paralleled by a rise in vulgar individualism and self-oriented, manipulative behavior. Community interests, the good of all, fragments into a divided melee of individual strategies and purposes. The shared social norms of the broader culture give way to a competitive, even predatory brand of individualism whereby selfish action in violation of sensible cultural codes of behavior becomes the typical counter-norm. Common goals and bonds are sacrificed in a culture dominated by consumer fetishes, the near-frenzied substitution of product worship and individual property ownership for more social goals of fellowship and equality. Within such a society or local community, the communal glue that holds individuals together in shared goals and modes of achieving those goals decays and crumbles. The individual feels unbounded and unguided. The individual lives an unsure existence lacking alliance to steady social norms or values.

Students who succeed within the demoralizing context of the level system climb the system's ladder through self-serving individualism. Many others who do not mount a sustained effort up the levels over many months become masters of manipulation and obfuscation. These so-called manipulators (a common term that denies the manipulative ethic taught by the system) twist and turn within the gaps and crevices of the system; ever seeking ways to get away with noncompliance without losing points, pull a fast one on a soft teacher who hesitates to fully enforce the system, or break the rules beyond the view of the teacher's vigilant eyes. Both success and subversive manipulation enact an instrumental individualism marking social decay, a

Machiavellian selfishness that fails to value the self just as it fails to consider the common bond.

Isolation

The experience of isolation is not merely temporary loneliness or friendlessness but a deep, hardened sense that one is an outcast, that one does not belong; moreover, that there is no belonging to be had. The isolated individual feels that, though she may be physically present with members of a community or group, she shares nothing with them, no identity, purpose, or values. Isolation, in this sense, is the dramatic and harsh experience of being distinctly outside and separate from the culture or community.

In the level system E/BD program, a central theme is the idea that one is working to return to the general education classroom through acts of compliance that earn points. The level system ladder is erected to propel a compliant student over the wall, back into the normal sphere. One is working to leave behind the community of deviants and defectives of which one is a member, thereby eclipsing one's stigmatized social identity through submission to authority.

Perhaps the ultimate form of isolation is to be part of a group that one is not supposed to identify with value or love. One is encouraged by the professionals to live in opposition to one's own peer group, one's own friends. One is encouraged to earn a place of normality by distancing oneself from the defective group. Even the act of winning is based on the loss of friendship, of shared value, of community. Losing one's disordered self requires a detachment and revulsion from one's peers.

Self-Estrangement

To be estranged from oneself is to become lost in activities and notions which deter or block the individual from constructing a self and livelihood of subjectively meaningful value. The estranged person is consumed in pursuits in which neither the activities, the self, nor the social group to which one identifies are understood to be morally valuable. The person is not maintained as valuable in and of himself. The person's actions are empty of subjective worth. Both the individual and the individual's actions gain meaning only as strategic maneuvers to bring about rewards that lie outside the individual's actions. The individual identity and effort are subsumed beneath the operational logic of other-directed, reward-seeking activity.

Following on the theme of isolation, we can see the compliant E/BD-labeled student striving to earn a place of normality by leaving himself and his community of peers behind. To Marx, estranged labor and alienated labor were synonymous. Estranged labor simultaneously exiles one from oneself and from the community of fellow humans through which one's actions take moral shape and gain social significance. Estrangement is the path of losing oneself, of losing humanity, the very death of the soul. For the student schooled in a level system, estrangement is a counter-developmental process, a detour from the typical childhood development toward the dialectic of individuation and community. The healthy developmental path calls for the growing child to simultaneously find and make himself as a thinking and responsible agent within the psychosocial tensions of allegiance and individuation, affiliation and agency. Ultimately and hopefully, the adolescent finds himself as unique and valuable amidst a social, communal context of family, friends, community, and humanity. The alienated path steers the developing child away from his own identity as a moral and social being, away from the very crucible of labor whereby the opportunity to create a moral self lies.

Conclusion: Are the Teachers Trapped, Too?

Although it is customary to end a critical essay by pointing to some optimistic light at the end of the tunnel, I am going to conclude by asking another question. It is troubling to me to realize that many caring and talented professionals who entered this profession in order to nurture the well-being of their students work within level systems. My question is: If level systems structure a social context in which student action is alienated labor and students experience these many dimensions of alienation, then how does such a context impact the hearts and minds of teachers? On the surface, it would seem that caring and devoted teachers simply would not participate in a process of demoralizing their students. In my experience, some teachers leave E/BD programs for just this reason. However, many stay and continue to work in this system. It would be simplistic for me to say that the truly caring teachers leave while the uncaring ones remain. The issue is far too complex for that kind of conclusion.

We have to ask ourselves how working in an alienating social environment affects teachers as well as students. Unfortunately, there is no research on this issue in relation to E/BD level system programs. However, we can turn to the work of LeCompte and Dworkin (1991) on the relationship between student disaffection and teacher burnout in urban schools. LeCompte and Dworkin (1991), in their analysis of the problems of urban schools, found that teachers and students alike experience an extreme degree of dissatisfaction and powerlessness in schools. A variety of sociological factors in urban schools strip teachers and students alike of their dignity, autonomy, power, and value, often turning the process of public education itself into an exercise in hopelessness and defeat. Although much of the Le-Compte and Dworkin (1991) analysis is not directly relevant to our purposes, one crucial insight is. These researchers connect the emotional and social well-being (or lack thereof) of the teachers with that of the students, explaining both as aspects of and outcomes of alienating social processes within the school. The level of satisfaction, engagement, interest, and hope experienced by the teachers is inseparable from those experienced by the students—and vice versa.

What does this mean for E/BD teachers? For those working in level systems, their daily participation in maintaining systems of social control that fail to meet the emotional and social needs of students is likely to be experienced by them as alienation. Their efforts fall far short of meeting the goals and ideals that they had hoped to fulfill by becoming a teacher, creating a gap between expectations and experienced realities. This gap leads to alienation in the five dimensions outlined above. While all teaching undoubtedly involves a gap between what we hope to contribute to the lives of our students and what we are actually able to do for them, between the sense of purpose and fulfillment we hope to experience for ourselves and the range of ups and downs that actually occurs, the teacher in the E/BD level system faces a gap of enlarged and amplified form. Often special education teachers enter this profession with a desire to connect with students, to build relationships that yield satisfaction, strength, and joy on both sides. Rightly, these teachers assume that such warm and deep relationships are the best of what professionals can offer to and create with students.

Level systems limit the actions of teachers and the interactions of teachers and students by effectively interposing a discourse of economic and behavioral compliance into the space of teacher-student relationships. The interactions that create and maintain these relationships are greatly structured by terms and priorities of the level system. The teacher views and talks to the student as the one to be held in compliance, while the student views and talks to the teacher as the one who appraises his actions as possible commodities with exchange value. The point and level system provides the roles and the vocabulary of compliance for each to use. Whatever moral or humanistic goals one might wish to seek within the teacher-student relationship itself, what many would claim is the most redeeming and important aspect of schooling for students experiencing emotional and social difficulties and their teachers, are subsumed by the goals of compliance and economic exchange.

I recall a discussion I once had with a graduate student who was student teaching in a level system school. He told me about a time when one of his students became very angry and pushed his book off his desk. The book fell to the floor. Despite all that he had been taught at the university, the student teacher did not to talk to this student about what was going on, about his thoughts, feelings, and actions. I asked the student teacher why he didn't talk to his student, for it seemed reasonable that a teacher in this situation could provide some emotional support and problem-solving guidance to the angry student. The student teacher replied, "I'm not allowed to do that. I have to process all of the student's behaviors through the point system." His hands were tied, he admitted sadly. Just as the system dictated the actions of the students, so too the system dictated his actions, framing his interactions with students in a way that limited how caring or supportive he could be. The level system limited who he could be as it restricted who his student could be, thereby limiting who they might become together. This, above all, is what Marx tried to teach us: to be aware of and rebel against social systems of our own construction that do not allow us to become responsible and able actors within the moral community of human relationships.

References

Axelos, K., & Bruzina, R. (1976). *Alienation, praxis, and techne in the thought of Karl Marx.* Austin: University of Texas Press.

Bauer, A. M., & Shea, T. M. (1988). Structuring classrooms through levels systems. *Focus on Exceptional Children, 21(3)*, 1–12.

Bauer, A. M., Shea, T. M., & Keppler, R. (1986). Levels systems: A framework for the individualization of behavior management. *Behavioral Disorders, 11,* 28–35.

Berlin, I. (1963). *Karl Marx: His life and environment.* New York: Oxford University Press.

Blatt, B. (1970). *Exodus from pandemonium; human abuse and a reformation of public policy.* Boston: Allyn & Bacon.

Blatt, B., & Kaplan, F. (1966). *Christmas in purgatory; a photographic essay on mental retardation.* Boston: Allyn & Bacon.

Calabrese, R. L. & Cochran, J. T. (1990). The Relationship of Alienation to Cheating among a Sample of American Adolescents. *Journal of Research & Development in Education, 23(2)*, 65–72.

Calabrese, R. L. & Poe, J. (1991). Alienation: An Explanation of High Dropout Rates among African American and Latino Students. *Educational Research Quarterly, 14(4)*, 22–26.

Danforth, S. (2000). Resistance theories: Exploring the politics of oppositional behavior. *Multiple Voices for Ethnically Diverse Learners*, 13–29.

Docking, J. (1990) *Education and alienation in the junior school*. New York: Falmer Press.

Erickson, K. (1986). On work and alienation. *American Sociological Review, 51(1)*, 1–8.

Foley, D. E. (1990). *Learning capitalist culture*. Philadelphia: University of Pennsylvania Press.

Fromm, E. (1961). *Marx's concept of man*. New York: Frederick Ungar.

Giroux, H. (1983). *Theory and resistance in education: A pedagogy for the opposition*. South Hadley, MA: Bergin and Garvey.

Goffman, E. (1961). *Asylums*. Garden City, NY: Anchor Books.

Gramsci, A. (1992). *The prison notebooks*. New York: Columbia University Press.

Hickerson, N. (1966) *Education for alienation*. Englewood Cliffs: Prentice-Hall.

Israel, J. (1971). *Alienation: From Marx to modern sociology*. Boston: Allyn & Bacon.

Kalekin-Fishman, D. (1996). Tracing the growth of alienation: Enculturation, socialization,and schooling in democracy. (pp. 95-106) In Geyer, F. (Ed.) *Alienation, ethnicity, and postmodernism*. Westport: Greenwood Press.

Knitzer, J., Steinberg, Z., & Fleisch, B. (1990). *At the schoolhouse door*. New York: Bank Street College of Education.

LeCompte, M. D, & Dworkin A. G. (1991). *Giving up on school: Student dropouts and teacher burnouts*. Newbury Park, CA: Corwin Press.

Leight, R. L. (1974). *Philosophers speak on alienation in education*. Danville: Interstate Printers & Publishers.

Liazos, A. (1978). School, Alienation, and Delinquency. *Crime & Delinquency. 24(3)*, 355-70.

Loken, J. O. (1973). *Student alienation and dissent*. Scarborough, Ontario: Prentice-Hall of Canada.

MacLeod, J. (1987). *Ain't no makin' it*. Boulder, CO: Westview Press.

Mannheim, K. (1940). *Man and society in an age of reconstruction; studies in modern social structure*. London : K. Paul, Trench, Trubner & Co.

Marcuse, H. (1964). *One dimensional man: Studies in the ideology of advanced industrial society*. Boston: Beacon Press.

Marx, K. (1964). *The economic and philosophic manuscripts of 1844*. New York: International Publishers.

——— (1990). *Capital*. Vol. 1. New York: Penguin.

McLaren, P. L. (1985). The ritual dimensions of resistance: Clowning and symbolic inversion. *Journal of Education, 167(2)*, 84–97.

——— (1993). *Schooling as a ritual performance*. New York: Routledge.

Meszaros, I. (1970). *Marx's theory of alienation*. London: Merlin Press.

Scheuermann, B. (1994). Level Systems and the Law: Are They Compatible? *Behavioral Disorders, 19(3)*, 205-20.

Seeman, M. (1959). On the meaning of alienation. *American Sociological Review, 24*, 783-791.

——— (1975). Alienation studies. *Annual Review of Sociology*, 1(9), 1-123.

——— (1979). Some themes in the alienation perspective: A commentary on Toch. *Journal of Community Psychology, 7(1)*, 12-17.

——— (1983). Alienation motifs in contemporary theorizing: The hidden continuity of the classic themes. *Social Psychology Quarterly, 46(3)*, 171-84.

Smith, S. W., & Farrell, D. T. (1993). Level system use in special education: Classroom intervention with prima facie appeal. *Behavioral Disorders, 18*(4), 251–264.

Stroul, B. (1996). *Children's mental health: Creating systems of care in a changing society.* Baltimore: Brookes.

Stroul, B., Lourie, I., Goldman, S., & Katz-Leavy, J. (1992). Profiles of local systems of care for children and adolescents with severe emotional disturbances. Washington, DC: Georgetown University Child Development Center, National Technical Assistance Center for Children's Mental Health.

West, C. (1991). *The ethical dimensions of Marxist thought.* New York: Monthly Review Press.

Williams, S. B. (1987) A comparative study of black dropouts and black high school graduates in an urban public school system. *Education & Urban Society, 19(3),* 311-19.

Willis, P. (1977). *Learning to labour.* Farnborough, England: Saxon House.

Woods, P. (1990). *The happiest days? How pupils cope with school.* New York: Falmer.

Zeeman, R. D. (1982) Creating change in academic self-concept and school behavior in alienated school students. *School Psychology Review, 11(4),* 459-61.

7 Many Possible Futures, Many Different Directions: Merging Critical Special Education and Disability Studies

Linda Ware

> Children can be provided with too constrained and impoverished a view of future possibilities...this can happen to any child...but it is a kind of harm to which those already afflicted with some measure of disability may be particularly liable.
>
> Alasdair MacIntyre (1999)

> Adah was the only one of us in our family with something wrong with her. But here nobody stares at Adah except just a little because she's white. Nobody cares that she's bad on one whole side because they've all got their own handicap children or mama with no feet, or their eye put out. When you take a look out the door, why, there goes somebody with something missing off of them and not even embarrassed of it. They'll wave a stump at you if they've got one, in a friendly way.
>
> *The Poisonwood Bible*, by Barbara Kingsolver (1990)

The literature emerging from disability studies, and particularly that from humanities-based disability studies, offers a way "in" to appeal to educators' aesthetic sensibilities. This interdisciplinary critical genre draws from scholarship in history, literature, philosophy, anthropology, religion, medical history, and rhetoric to re-create a developed portrait of disabled people across histories and cultures. Clearly, disability studies offers a plot that differs from that of special education, one that speaks to the humanity that we share rather than the one that estranges and others our differences. Therefore, I am less interested in crafting a normative framework for disability studies in education, as it suggests "absorption" of this rich field of scholarship. Rather, I urge that disability studies scholars in education explore this literature and creatively integrate this new perspective joining in solidarity with other academics who have accepted the challenge to rewrite the discourse that defines disability.

In this chapter I consider possible linkages for critical special education and humanities-based disability studies. I draw from selected disability studies scholarship that complements the decades-old criticism by critical special educators who have challenged the well-entrenched culture of traditional special education. Merging these two discourses on disability both intensifies the critique of the traditional paradigm of special education and strengthens our alliances within academia to restory special education and disability. Throughout this chapter I weave examples of an integrative approach characterized in my own research and teaching, writing as a critical special education theorist who has joined forces with disability studies scholars to rewrite the discourse that defines disability.

Critical special education provides a critique of the normative practices, beliefs, and assumptions about disability outlined in the bulk of the traditional special education literature. Although the term is rarely used in textbooks or traditional special education journals to distinguish traditional from critical perspectives, individuals, including Doug Biklen, Burton Blatt, Phillip M. Ferguson, Lous Heshusius, Richard Iano, Mary Poplin, Thomas M. Skrtic, Steve Taylor, and more recently Ellen Brantlinger, Deb Gallagher, Susan Gabel, Scot Danforth, Nirmella Erevelles, and myself are among those who contribute to this scholarship. Among the many European contributors are Julie Allan, Keith Ballard, Len Barton, Tony Booth, Fazil Rizvi, Roger Slee, and Sally Tomlinson.

Readers who claim, without apology, critical special education status—rabid, vigilante, coercive, or otherwise—remain conflicted (if not perplexed) by the unalterable mechanisms of traditional special education. Some have grown weary in the struggle and moved into various other worlds such as critical studies, cultural foundations, critical social theory, or perhaps they have relocated to general education. Migration to these new spaces has inspired writing from alternative discourses in a persistent attempt to find a "way out" of traditional special education thought and practice. However, within these alternative fields of inquiry, efforts to link intellectual forces within a wider academic audience to address educational, economic, and social injustice targeted at disabled people has yet to occur. Borrowing from Roger Slee (1997), "people are not of themselves disabled, [being disabled] is a relational concept within a sociological discourse rather than a pathological descriptor within a medical discourse" (p. 175).

Elsewhere I describe the failure of critical theorists to consider disability related issues, noting that although many critical special education theorists borrow from this literature, disability occupies little more than sideshow status extraneous to the "big tent" concerns of critical theorists (see also Erevelles, 2000; Gabel, 2001; Ware, 2001a).

Similar exclusion remains in general education teacher preparation. Despite the success of a few universities across the United States that have abandoned the dual system of teacher preparation, most have failed to imagine possibilities beyond the parameters of inherited institutional practice (Blanton, Griffin, Winn, & Pugach, 1997). The tensions in schools of education specific to disability and "inclusive education" parallel those in K–12 settings where educators are constrained by institutional structures that insure exclusion and where cultural barriers obscure alternative understandings of disability. Inclusive education is used as in the European context in which the term aims to expose the fundamental nature of "exclusive" education. In this way, inclusion is the work of both general and special education (see Ballard, 1999).

Despite the fact that the majority of schools of education do not adhere to the minimal tenets of inclusive education practice within their own institutions, they continue to devise interventions in support of K–12 inclusion and clamor for best practices despite being wholly unqualified to the task (Ware, in press). Such contradiction in practice was explored as complicity in the instance of racial inequity in colleges of education that unwittingly perpetuate and prop up institutionally sanctioned "cycles of oppression" (Lawrence & Tatum cited in Cochran-Smith, 2000). In the example of disability, similar cycles of oppression emerge once faculty confront inherent institutional contradictions. In a recent research funded by the National Endowment for the Humanities (Ware, 2000), humanities faculty and colleagues in the school of medicine considered the development of disability studies curriculum only to be stymied by similar tensions that challenged the integrity of programmatic changes (Ware, in press).

Although solidarity across a wider academic community will be essential to the success of disability studies in education, the greater challenge remains special education's behaviorist tradition—the ghost that haunts the stories told about disability and education. Behaviorist orthodoxy threatens the potential for alliances we might otherwise form as the frame is fixed on disability as a story of pathologizing difference in pursuit of normalization. Although critical special educators are familiar with the long history of efforts to displace behaviorism and positivist inquiry that has shaped the discourse on disability in education, many educators lack this knowledge. This history of the "disappeared" includes scholars from both sides of the Atlantic as well as Australia and New Zealand who are excluded from special education's traditional knowledge base. Lous Heshusius provides a similar analysis of North American scholarship she characterized as the "four waves of discontent" in the field of special education (Heshusius, 2000). A brief overview of this rich and worthy history is provided in the section that follows so that readers can appreciate the potential for linking critical special education scholarship with the emerging work in disability studies.

Critical Special Education's Discontent, Discordant, and Disappeared

Burton Blatt was among the earliest critics of special education doctrine rooted in technical and scientific progress and its potential to ameliorate the problems of mentally disabled persons. His efforts to expose social injustice and acts of inhumanity towards disabled people inspired his 1966 book, *Christmas in Purgatory* (with photographs by Fred Kaplan), and the subsequent photographic expose that appeared in *Look* magazine (1967). These works quickly raised public awareness of the historically inhumane treatment of disabled people and became instrumental in the deinstitutionalization movement of the 1970s. As a lifelong educator, Blatt was a strong advocate for those he viewed as the most "abused of the abused, the least able to advocate for themselves and the most in need of advocates" (1970, p. xvi). Decades later when Blatt retired as Dean of the School of Education at the University of Syracuse, he had authored more than 300 articles, chapters, and books, and published a range of works including poetry and fiction in addition to research articles, essays, and monographs.

More recently, Blatt was acknowledged by colleagues as the inspiration for the emergence of disability studies (Bogdan, 2000), and yet in a recently published collection of papers, Seymour Sarason (1999) lamented:

> In the last decade I have had occasion to observe many special-class programs in public schools. In my talks with special-class teachers and administrators I would always seek in some way to bring up Burt's name, if only in an effort to indicate that I was knowledgeable about the field. Aside from the few usual exceptions, Burt's name was not known to most of them. I found and still find that incomprehensible. Regardless of our field, we all need and should have role models and heroes. At the very least I expect a professional to know the history of his or her field, because without such knowledge one's own sense of professional identity is an impoverished one. (p. xviii)

Although Sarason's point is well taken, he erroneously assumed that Blatt was actually represented in the special education orthodoxy. Burton Blatt was among the early discordant voices silenced by the regime of special education traditionalists who have long manipulated the field's official knowledge base and have either misappropriated or completely misunderstood Blatt's legacy (Brantlinger, 1997). Then as now, the special education knowledge base remains grounded in a functionalist behaviorist tradition that views truth as singular, relies on a microscopic view of human nature, employs social science methods, and through analysis of causal factors places a high premium on prediction and control to yield law-like generalizations. Gallagher (1998) provides a thorough analysis of the misinterpretation of science in special education suggesting in her pointed criticism:

> Masquerading under the guise of science, this knowledge base, or more accurately, the scientistic version of empiricism that produced it, can neither provide the foundation for nor sustain adequate reforms in special education. (499)

Lous Heshusius has remained vigilant in her critique of special education orthodoxy citing four waves as "illustrative of the movement of discontent" (Heshusius, in press). The first wave began in the late 1960s with Burton Blatt (1966) and Robert Edgerton (1967) and extended into the 1970s with the publication of an alternative special education textbook edited by Blatt, Biklen, and Bogdan (1977). This progressive era also challenged issues of assessment and labeling by Gerald Coles (1978), and more humane approaches to understanding emotional disabilities suggested by William Rhodes (1974). The second wave occurred in the 1980s launched by proponents of holism, including Lous Heshusius (1982, 1986), Richard Iano (1986, 1990), and Mary Poplin (1987, 1988a, 1988b). Their claims were enhanced by the sociological critiques offered by James Carrier (1983), Christine Sleeter (1986), and Sally Tomlinson (1982). Also included in this era were Mehen, Hertweck, and Meihls (1986), who published the first critical ethnography on special education in the context of schools. The third wave was characterized by interpretivists, activists, and postmodernists, including Keith Ballard (1994), Phil and Diane Ferguson and Steve Taylor (1992), Michael Oliver (1992), and Tom Skrtic (1991). Finally, in the present moment, the fourth wave draws from a disparate group of scholars, who have begun to influence the nascent field of disabilities studies in education (Ballard, 1999; Baker, 2002; Danforth, 1997; Erevelles, 2000; Gabel, 1999; Slee, 1997; Ware, 2001a; 2002; Ware, forthcoming).

Heshusius is hopeful that special education's long-standing model for "prevention/treatment/remediation/measurement" will finally be abandoned in pursuit of a "social/cultural/political" understanding of disability linked to academia's growing interest in disability studies. I, too, share this optimism, with the extended hope that educators' attitudes, assumptions, and beliefs about disability can be enriched by this emerging interdisciplinary scholarship. If we can articulate a place for disability studies in both general and special education, we can change the story "so far" of special education. By that I mean to say that exposure to and engagement with this new field of inquiry could interrupt the "authorized" silence among educators specific to the relationship between unexamined schooling practices and the material reality of disability in society. Although Tom Skrtic (1991) reasoned that special educators lacked the theoretical background to engage in self-critique given their long history of ignoring criticism that emerged from the outside and condemning the criticism that emerged from the inside—as in the example of critical special education (p. 58). I suggest here that the critique emerging from disability studies need not provoke antipathy. Further into this chapter I describe how this literature captivates students, teachers, and administrators and prompts self-reflection about whom we "other" and how we "other" in society at large and schools, in particular.

Thus, the articulation of disability studies in education assumes, first, solidarity across academic disciplines; second, recovery of the discordant voices of critical special educators; and third self-critique among general and special educators to generate an "explicit and sustained analysis" of the educational treatment of disabled people (Rizvi & Christensen, 1996, p. 2). In the absence of such critical analysis educators will continue to deny the intrusive paternalism of the existing system, disbelieve that the system reinforces stereotypes of dependence and inferiority, dismiss the logic of the social construction of disability, and dispute their own complicity in pathologizing disability.

For a Foucauldian analysis of the construction of regimes of power, including those maneuvered by disabled and nondisabled students in a secondary setting, see, e.g., Allan (1999). Brantlinger (1997) provides a comprehensive critique of the status of special education orthodoxy, whereas Corbett (1996) Skrtic (1991), Slee (1997), Tomlinson (1982), and Ware (2001b) reveal the unwitting complicity among insiders who pathologize disability.

Restorying Special Education

The *Handbook on Disability Studies* (2001) edited by Gary L. Albrecht, Katherine D. Seelman, and Michael Bury, is a useful resource from which to launch the restorying of special education. Educators new to the topic of disability studies—and those who are familiar with this critical new scholarship—will find the collection essential reading. The *Handbook* is organized in three sections that capture the multiple perspectives and the multiparadigmatic nature of disability studies: Part I: *The Shaping of Disability Studies as a Field*, Part II: *Experiencing Disability*, and Part III: *Disability in Context*. Given the scope of this scholarship, it should become apparent why it is less important, at this time, to develop a single definition or normative framework to disability studies specific to education. Two reasons merit a more considered explication below—that of the field's interdisciplinary aims and the international applications.

First, given the field's interdisciplinary origins in the social sciences, humanities, and rehabilitation science efforts have just begun to bridge these fairly complex boundaries in pursuit of integrative approaches to develop a coherent field of inquiry. Disciplinary distinctions, divisions, subdivisions, and departments characterize the existing structure of higher education and simultaneously pose the greatest obstacles to responsive teaching in the twenty-first century. According to the former Dean of the College of Humanities at the University of Arizona, Annette Kolodny (1998), the future of higher education in the twenty-first century will be determined by recognition of an increasingly heterogeneous student body whose future problems will consist of "complexly interwoven challenges" ranging from racial and ethnic hatred to the radical destruction of biological habitats (p. 40). Unfortunately, the fragmented order of inherited institutions of higher education will no longer serve to address such problems given that they tend to fall outside singular, narrow disciplines of knowledge. Kolodny and others propose that the only way to move forward will be to create *genuinely* interdisciplinary programs. This effort will likely prove arduous in academia where "there are no reward systems for change and no incentives to be bold, visionary, or experimental" (p. 210). Despite the obvious challenges posed by interdisciplinarity, disability studies scholars believe the field will mature as "theory, concepts, appreciation of differences, and acknowledgement of political implications are refined and incorporated into the discourse" (Albrecht, Seelman, & Bury, 2001, p. 3). Clearly, educators must have a stake in this articulation.

Second, in the example of international applications of an integrative approach to disability studies, there exists a legitimate complexity of contextual representations of disability bound by international borders that will necessitate a circumspect analysis of the historical, economic, social, value, and institutional issues within a given country. Much debate has occurred between those who support a social model of disability versus those who endorse a rights model. These debates have decreased somewhat, but they are nevertheless useful for readers to review.

Thus, to view disability through a cultural lens begs the questions: Which culture? Which lens? And to what ends? The *Handbook* attempts to broaden the field of disability studies by including interdisciplinary and international scholarship and for these reasons I suggest that educators engage with this literature and reflect upon its relationship to their own areas of interest (see the subsequent section). Because this literature can enrich our efforts to restory special education and disability, I urge that we avoid the temptation to simply "pour old wine into new bottles." Disability studies in education cannot become the morphed successor of critical special education. We must work through the articulation of this scholarship among ourselves and with others who value genuinely interdisciplinary programs.

A Collaborative Inquiry on Disability

> In the societies where Western science and medicine are powerful culturally, and where their promise to control nature is still widely believed, people with disabilities are constant reminders of the failures of that promise, and of the inability of science and medicine to protect everyone from illness, disability, and death. They are "the Others" that science would like to forget. In the societies where there are strong ideals of bodily perfection to which everyone is supposed to aspire, people with disabilities are the imperfect "Others" who can never come close enough to the ideals; identifying with them would remind the non-disabled that their ideals imply a degree of control that must eventually elude them too. (Wendell, 1996, p. 63)

In this section I describe research supported by the National Endowment for the Humanities (NEH) that enabled both secondary and postsecondary faculty to consider the meaning of disability as a concept and a constituency (Ware, 2000). The project consisted of three components: first, a disability studies lecture series; second, six collaborative inquiry dialogues for university faculty and secondary teachers to consider possible ways to integrate disability-related content into their teaching; and third, planning time for the general and special educators to discuss selected disability readings and the lecture themes in preparation to integrate this content into their teaching (Ware, 2001a; 2001b, Ware, 2002; Ware, forthcoming). The lectures included: *Seeing the Disabled: Visual Rhetorics in Popular Photography* (Rosemarie Garland-Thomson), *Representation and Its Discontents* (David T. Mitchell & Sharon L. Snyder), *Seeing Invisible Disabilities: Reading the Romantic Body in Medical Practice* (Stephanie Brown-Clark), *Cultures of Piety and the*

Moral Meaning of Disability in the United States (Nancy L. Eiseland), *Caring, Justice and Disability* (Eva F. Kittay), and *The Withering Away of the Disability State: A Possible Future for Disability Studies* (Lennard J. Davis). Selected readings from Michael Berube (1996), Tom Couser (1997), Simi Linton (1998), Nancy Mairs (1996), and more popular works as in the example of Eli Claire (1999), John Hockenberry (1995), and others. Also included were documentary films: *Disability Culture Rap* (Wade, 2000); *Vital Signs: Crip Culture Talks Back* (Snyder & Mitchell, 1996); and *When Billy Broke His Head... and Other Tales of Wonder* (Golfus & Simpson, 1994).

Teachers found the complex and layered view of disability presented in the lectures and in our readings unfamiliar and yet fascinating. Although disability permeates the everyday schooling context in multiple and complex ways, it is the medical model alone that inscribes ideology, history, social, and political assumptions about disability. Conversations about the meaning of the concept of disability are rare among educators who generally accept the categorical definitions of disability proffered by special education systems that, in turn, displace the lived experience and thus diminish understanding disability as part of the larger human experience. The received narratives of disability, as Wendell and others suggest, reside at the level of unconscious thought and as such often remain uninterrogated. This project provided time for discussion of disability as a product of cultural rather than biological forces inviting a range of "bewildering" responses—as one teacher characterized the discussions, the point being that it was bewildering to find how certain emotions around the unspoken topic of disability "cut both ways." Shame, for example, while often expressed by disabled people, was also expressed by nondisabled people, shamed by their lack of understanding or reticence to engage with disabled people. This observation is similar to the analysis offered by Beverly Tatum (1992) when teachers talk about race.

The content we explored was unknown to the participants as was the larger movement to integrate disability studies in higher education. As a consequence, the literature invoked rather than provoked new ways to think about disability on both personal and professional levels. Individual analyses of this literature prompted questions about the self in relation to the other that were either formerly overlooked or silenced. Some wondered why they had failed to think about disability as an identity marker, why empathy, anger, and resentment ultimately intersect in this literature, and why fear and pity were such prevalent themes. Others raised concerns about their own personal authority to introduce disability issues in their teaching, uncertain about where their students make take the topic (see Ware, 2001a for elaboration on this point).

Furthermore, teachers wondered why their teacher training never "really tackled this aspect of disability." According to one veteran teacher, "How we relate to one another around difference—well, it really never comes up. The assumption is, we should just know."

I Am Telling You About Disability

Throughout the NEH project, the teachers expressed awe at the multiple interpretations given to disability and its place in our lives as reflected in the lectures and materials we reviewed. Approaching disability from a humanities perspective suggests to some the potential for society to more fully understand disability, and therefore, to teach more rich and varied accounts of living with disability. The project seemed timely as K–12 classrooms, like society, have become more heterogeneous than at any time in the past. What was less obvious was how to initiate a cultural studies project such as this at a time when K–12 curricula were becoming increasingly standardized and calls for evidence-based research prevailed. It was, however, the perfect moment to question what "evidence" mattered.

The accounts of lived experience depicted in the materials we examined underscored the theoretical analysis presented in the lectures, but also engaged the teachers on a personal level. Eli Claire's autobiography, *Exile & Pride: Disability, Queerness, and Liberation* (1999) was among the most powerful works for the participants. Like Berube, Mairs, and others, Claire made purposeful connections to theory and lived experience as in the example below from which I quote at length.

> For as long as I can remember, I have avoided certain questions. Would I have been a good runner if I didn't have CP? Could I have been a surgeon or pianist, a dancer or gymnast? Tempting questions that have no answers. I refuse to enter the territory marked *bitterness*. I wondered about a friend who calls herself one of the last of the polio tribe, born just before the polio vaccine's discovery. Does she ever ask what her life might look like had she been born five years later? On a topological map, bitterness would be outlined in red.

> I thought about the model of disability that separates impairment from disability. Disability theorist Michael Oliver defines impairment as "lacking part of or all of a limb, or having a defective limb, organism or mechanism of the body." I lack a fair amount of fine motor control. My hands shake. I can't play a piano, place my hands gently on a keyboard, or type even 15 words a minute. Whole paragraphs never cascade from

my fingertips. My long hand is a slow scrawl. I have trouble picking up small objects, putting them down. Dicing onions with a sharp knife puts my hands at risk. A food processor is not a yuppie kitchen luxury in my house, but an adaptive device. My gross motor skills are better but not great. I can walk mile after mile, run and jump and skip and hop, but don't expect me to walk a balance beam. A tightrope would be murder; boulder hopping and rock climbing, not much better. I am not asking for pity. I am telling you about impairment.

Oliver defines disability as "the disadvantage or restriction of activity caused by a contemporary social organization which takes no or little account of people who have physical (and/or cognitive/developmental/mental) impairments and thus excludes them from the mainstream of society." I write slowly enough that cashiers get impatient as I sign my name to checks, stop talking to me, turn to my companions, hand them my receipts. I have failed timed tests, important tests, because teachers wouldn't allow me extra time to finish the sheer physical act of writing, wouldn't allow me to use a typewriter. I have been turned away from jobs because my potential employer believed my slow, slurred speech meant I was stupid. Everywhere I go people stare at me, in restaurants as I eat, in grocery stores as I fish coins out of my pocket to pay the cashier, in parks as I play with my dog. I am not asking for pity. I am telling you about disability.

I decided that Michael Oliver's model of disability makes theoretical and political sense but misses important emotional realities. (pp 5-7, from *Exile & Pride: Disability, Queerness, and Liberation*, 1999, with permission from South End Press.)

Although Eli Claire focuses on current experiences as an adult, teachers speculated about her school experience drawing comparisons to their own students. Others wondered: *How different was the cashier's response to that of a teacher? Could I be that cashier? Could I be Eli Claire?* Informed by this literature and our discussions, teachers were more willing to contest the view of disability being deeply etched in education with its emphasis on "individual" problems renamed pathology. Claire refuses individual pathology, and instead pathologizes the built environment and the culture and systems that sustain it. In some ways, it was a relief for the teachers to acknowledge the contradictions in systems other than education and to concede that they were not the only gatekeepers in society. However, it was troubling to contend with the fact that difference poses a dilemma in our culture. According to legal scholar Martha Minow (1990), this is symptomatic of a "particular" way of looking at the world one in which "the problem arises only in a culture that officially condemns the assigned status of inequalities and yet, in practice, perpetuates them" (p. 79). Our readings and discussions brought into sharp relief the subtle influence of ideology and the power of a given paradigm to "treat" disability rather than to allow that the experience be viewed as an integral part of humanity.

Why Do We Have to Think About Disability?

Throughout this research I was struck by the absence of the often asked questions, *Why do we have to do inclusion? I don't teach special education so why do I have to think about disability?* This point merits elaboration for several reasons. First, my approach to working with schools in support of inclusive education has consistently encouraged general and special educators to interrogate institutional incentives that preserve the status quo. Often, the process becomes contentious once the participants make bold connections to social injustice performed in schools and then they must choose to either disrupt or accept the consequences of ignoring everyday acts of injustice in schools. In addition to the critical special education scholarship cited earlier, I also borrow extensively from international inclusive education research and scholarship. Taken together, this literature provides an incisive critique of conventional approaches succinctly articulated by Jenny Corbett and Roger Slee (2000).

> Inclusive education is a distinctly political "in your face" activity that proceeds from larger political, as opposed to technical questions about the nature of society and the status afforded to people in varying forms and structures of social organization. A political movement in the first instance, inclusion is about establishing access for all people. It is not conditional, nor does it speak about partial inclusion. Its impetus emanates from the recipients of professional services rather than from being orchestrated by professionals themselves. (p. 136)

Their analysis, when juxtaposed to the frequently cited versions of inclusion offered by Stainback & Stainback (1990) and Lipsky & Gartner (1996) reveals how federally financed research in special education has trivialized the education of students with disabilities by ignoring its clear political aspects. Sadly, this depoliticized approach to inclusion has impacted the global research agenda, which Slee (2001) has characterized as driven by five basic questions: (1) How do we refine our diagnostic tools to see what is exactly wrong with this child? (2) How is it manifested? (3) Under what conditions can we stem the disruptions it causes to the learning of the child and others? (4) How do we create the correct attitudes in schools to make sure that the child is accepted? (5) How do we ensure the correct mix of resources, expertise, and personnel support to facilitate the placement of the child? (p. 173).

For Slee this limited vision amounts to little more than "conservative incrementalism" that has reduced the research imperative to the "normalization of difference by stabilizing the newcomer in an environment that provides a buffer to enable schools to remain the same" (p. 173). Readers may recognize allusions to the critique of professional culture and school organization outlined by Tom Skrtic in which he characterized the futility of attempting change in resistant structures that later prompted his arguments for *adhocratic* rather than bureaucratic school organizations (1989, 1991). Equally apparent is the critique offered by Lous Heshusius (1982) in discussion of the "mechanistic view of reality" where

> Teaching and learning are reduced to the level of rules and instrumentality, the most subordinate level in the hierarchy of ways by which we know. Because of the required quantification and measurement, teaching and learning often do not operate at the levels of what is meaningful to the child and what is worthwhile in the first place. (p. 7)

At the time Heshusius published this very article I was a special education teacher working with Latino middle-school students in the community in which I was raised. As a resource teacher, the expectation for my students was the attainment of a "skills set" of hierarchically ranked routines matched to a grade-level curriculum that color-coded various levels of content. In short, the diagnostic-prescriptive approach I was compelled to follow for students who had a long history of *disengagement* with education systems ensured that the resource room was far from a resource for them. I read Heshusius' article with wild delight, astonished by her claims to link special education with more progressive thinking about knowledge in fields such as physics, biology, chemistry, astronomy, psychology, and educational research. Drawing on these alternative discourses, she urged educators to consider how, despite our best intentions, traditional special education practices "othered" students and alienated teachers from more humane interactions. Heshusius, unabashedly, questioned:

> Why do we seem compelled to perceive the measured effect, the rules, the techniques, as ends in themselves when, as professionals and human beings, our real concern is with the child? The answer lies in a view of reality that pervades our culture and that we take for granted, as if no other view could exist. (p. 7)

Specific to the consequences for teachers she asserted:

> In special education, our obsession with task analyses, behavioral objec-
> tives, and training of isolated skills (often in isolated settings) has led us
> to believe that discrete procedures will lead the student back to the
> whole, from which the steps were broken down in the first place. (p. 10)

Her criticism was explicit:

> [T]eachers cannot act in a professional and intelligent manner, for much
> is forbidden, much prescribed, and much so rigid that personal initia-
> tive is impossible. (p. 11).

Although positivism prevails in special education, I have consistently
utilized the work of these critical special educators along with the essays on
holism by Mary Poplin (1984) in my research and teaching. This critical
scholarship and that previously cited represents the earliest critique in support of the social model of disability among special educators. However, at
the time, the field could not intellectually respond when learning problems
were described as "interactions between the school, the individual student,
and society at large" (Poplin, p. 290). The field was again vexed by Skrtic's
(1991) argument that the institutional practice of special education and "the
very notion of student disability are artifacts of the functionalist quest for
rationality, order, and certainty in the field of education" (p. 44). Unfortunately, contemporary assumptions that fix behaviorism as the foundation for
special education remain among educators who never wholly understood
the meaning of the social construction of disability in the first place. Perhaps
the poetry of Eli Claire and others who provide first-person narratives of
disability along with the critical analyses emerging from disability studies in
the humanities will enhance our efforts to *restory* special education and disability. In so doing, we render unconscionable the question, *Why do I have to
think about disability?*

When Will We Come to Understand,
Value, and Teach Disability?

The degree to which disabled people have been stigmatized or oppressed as a consequence of particular cultural and historical eras' bias toward disabled people has proven to be one of the most critical topics of

interrogation by disability studies scholars in the humanities. In his introduction to *The Disability Studies Reader* (1997), Lennard J. Davis wrote that:

> People with disabilities have been isolated, incarcerated, observed, written about, operated on, instructed, implanted, regulated, treated, institutionalized, and controlled to a degree probably unequal to that experienced by any other minority group. (p. 1)

With this collective history, the call to reimagine disability may seem inadequate to the task before us. Even so, with so many varied insights emerging from disability studies, educators may indeed begin to imagine disability otherwise as we find ways to integrate these perspectives into our research and teaching. This chapter began with an epigraph from Alasdair MacIntyre, the moral philosopher who has only recently engaged disability in *Dependent Rational Animals: Why Human Beings Need the Virtues* (1999). For MacIntyre this text is a work of "correction" to expand his earlier analysis, which completely failed to address disability. Critical of the unjustifiable silence of moral philosophers to consider disability (including his own previous attempts to give an account of the place of virtues in our lives, see *After Virtue*, 1981), his revised analysis of moral virtues is now explicit about disability. In his view, "unrestricted imagination" will be necessary to move beyond the constrained and impoverished view of disability held by many in our society. In critical self-reflection, he explained, "by not reckoning adequately with this central feature of human life (disability) I had necessarily failed to notice some other important aspects of the part that the virtues play in human life" (p. x). The virtues he considers for self-making explicit to disability raise questions about the meaning of human vulnerability, the origins of flourishing and alternative futures, and concerns for whose good is considered in the common good. He holds that disabled children may have been denied "alternative realistic futures" or because of inadequate education denied the right to "imagine alternative possibilities" (p. 75). However, he calls on humanity to move beyond our complicity with the past and with both new knowledge and imagination to create the kind of community to develop the virtues. In his own words:

> How we structure our understanding of the future depends in part of course on the established uses of clocks, calendars, and modes of scheduling of the culture in which we find ourselves. But as a practical reason I have to be able to *imagine* different possible futures for me, to imagine myself moving forward from the starting point of the present in different directions. For *different or alternative futures* present me with different possible modes of flourishing. And it is important that I

should be able to envisage both nearer and more distant futures and to attach probabilities, even if only in a rough and ready way, to the future results of acting in one way rather than another. For this both knowledge and imagination are necessary.

MacIntyre's effort to explicitly address disability parallels other well-respected philosophers, including Anita Silvers, Eva F. Kittay, and Martha Nussbaum, who also call for new ways to reflect on the meaning of disability in our lives. Silvers, a prolific opponent of "special" rights for disabled people, argues in favor of the constitutional right to "be in the world" (tenBroek, 1966) and thus to be afforded basic civil rights rather than "special" rights (Francis & Silvers, 2000). Silvers demonstrates how so-called entitlements made to disabled people often fail to take into consideration consequences in the form of isolation that compound disadvantage (Silvers, Wasserman, & Mahowold, 1998). Her arguments would greatly inform decision making about service provision and delivery in schools that MacIntyre suggests currently comprise the "modes of scheduling the culture" (ibid).

Eva Kittay (1998) borrows from personal experience as a mother to ground her philosophical arguments about interdependence and connectedness between disabled and nondisabled people. She has described how her adult daughter with severe disabilities engages with others in unique and challenging ways to communicate and create relationships. Kittay, like MacIntyre, questions the meaning of dependency and how it has been misconstrued as the apex of virtue in western societies. In her view, until we free ourselves from our obsession with independence, we will continue to feel threatened by disabled people because they remind us of our own potential for dependency. Her aim is to "find a knife sharp enough to cut through the myth of dependence" (1999, p. xiii).

Finally, Martha Nussbaum recently recounted her nephew's experience with autism as a resource for understanding the meaning of social justice, disability, dependency, and the abelist assumptions of mutual advantage inherent in America's social contract tradition (2001). In an essay that appeared in the New York Review of Books, Nussbaum borrows from Berube (1999) to urge that greater imagination might promote a "more capacious and supple sense of what it means to be human" (as cited in Nussbaum, 2001). Michael Berube writes of his son Jaime, who has Down syndrome, to explain that it was imagination of a different sort that once enabled society to justify the institutionalization of the "mongoloid idiot"—a being essentialized beyond particular meaning and cast within a category of the "retarded." Nussbaum suggested that "it ought to be possible to learn to put in its place the image of Jaime, a particular child" (p. 37).

The critical analyses of these philosophers clearly extend the possibility to rewrite the discourse of disability and to merge theoretical and personal insights as urged by the editors (Kittay, Silvers, & Wendell) in the two-part special issue of *Hypatia: A Journal of Feminist Philosophy* in 2001 and 2002. Many teachers would bring a wealth of insight to a philosophical exploration of disability—both as students and in the authorship of more rich accounts of experiences with their students.

Sources of the Particular

In an address before an audience of administrators to introduce a research project in their district, *Understanding Disability and Transforming Schools*, (Ware, 2000), I posed the question: *When will we come to understand, value, and teach disability?* The question was received with silence, perplexing many in this audience who, much like a general audience, found such a notion challenged many core assumptions about disability. However, as professionals, given their frequent interactions with disability, how have school administrators and educators retained such a limited view of disability? I continued with an overview of disability studies contrasted to the construction of disability by special education. I pressed the audience to then define disability and to list values that might be associated with living with disability. Most were struck by the difficulty of this seemingly simple task. The excerpt by Lennard J. Davis above then served as a prompt for small group discussion in which both professional and personal insights emerged.

Like the teachers in the NEH project, these administrators had never considered disability through a cultural lens. Certainly schools do not interrogate the received messages of disability in which discourses of cure, care and compliance prevail—as if the way things are is given and immutable, with no need to seek out alternative meanings (Heshusius, 1982; Minow, 1990, see especially pp. 373–390). Disability studies scholarship can serve as the impetus for educators to contemplate the existence of stigma and disability in schools and society, to discuss its genesis, and to interrupt its reification in order to understand that disability is about more than the dilemmas it poses to schools. Because this literature speaks to our shared humanity, such an approach discourages the reprisal that can accompany contested debates about inclusion.

Conclusion

The integrative approach I have described here is just one interpretation of how educators might link disability studies scholarship with education. It is my belief that educators' attitudes, assumptions, and beliefs about disability can be enriched by humanities-based disability studies scholarship. However, such a goal must privilege the benefits for children—those who have been limited by "too constrained and impoverished view of future possibilities" (MacIntyre, 1999, p. 75). If disability is viewed as encompassing more than the dilemmas it poses in schools and in society, then as educators we will have to teach the value of disability in our lives. Albrecht, Seelman, & Bury (2001) suggest we view disability as both a private and public experience, one that assumes defining and redefining its meaning. They state,

> For some, disability represents a personal catastrophe to be avoided if at all possible, a shameful condition to be denied or hidden if present and negotiated within the sanctuary of one's family and personal space. For others, disability is a source of pride and empowerment—a symbol of enriched self-identity and self-worth and a central force coalescing a community intent on extolling the fundamental values of life, human rights, citizenship, and the celebration of difference. Disability for many reasons is a redefining experience, adding value to individual lives and clarifying what it means to be human. (p. 1)

K–12 schools must accept the challenge that disability studies present, and they must begin to include disability as a sense of "pride and empowerment." This chapter reveals how much remains to be done in an effort to persuade educators to move beyond the narrow view of disability inscribed by professional training and reified in everyday practice. Only then will educators begin to reconceptualize the curriculum so that in fact, disability matters in more meaningful ways to both teachers and to their students. The focus on disability shifts from dilemma to "difference that enriches society and creates new sets of powerful social bonds, responsibilities, and opportunities for individuals, families, and society" (Crozet et al., cited in Albrecht, Seelman, & Bury, 2001).

References

Albrecht, G. L., Seelman, K. D., & Bury, M. (2001). *Handbook of disability studies.* Thousand Oaks: Sage.
Allan, J. (1999). *Desperately seeking inclusion.* London: Falmer.

Baker, B. (2002). The hunt for disability: The new eugenics and the normalization of school children. *Teachers College Record, 104(4)*, 663–703.

Ballard, K. (1994). *Disability, family, whanau and society*. Palmerston, New Zealand: Dunmore Press.

———— (1999). *Inclusive education: International voices on disability and justice*. London: Falmer.

Berube, M. (1996). *Life as we know it: A father, a family, and an exceptional child*. New York: Vintage-Random House.

———— (1999, May). *Disability and the "difference" it makes*. Paper presented at the Smithsonian National Museum conference, Disability and the Practice of Public History, Washington, DC.

Blanton, L. P., Griffin, C. C., Winn, J. A., & Pugach, M.C. (1997). *Teacher education in transition: Collaborative programs to prepare general and special education educators*. Denver: Love Publishing Company.

Blatt, B., & Kaplan, F. (1966). *Christmas in purgatory: A photographic essay on mental retardation*. New York: Allyn and Bacon.

Blatt, B., Biklen, D., & Bogdan, R. (Eds.). (1977). *An alternative textbook in special education*. Denver: Love Publishing Company.

Bogdan, R. (2000, October). Disability studies at the crossroads. Keynote address at the Disability Studies conference, Syracuse University, Syracuse, NY.

Brantlinger, E. (1997). Using ideology: Cases of nonrecognition of the politics of research and practice in special education. *Review of Educational Research, 67(4)*, 425–459.

Carrier, J. G. (1983). Masking the social in educational knowledge: The case of learning disability theory. *American Journal of Adolescent Research, 9(3)*, 384–407.

Claire, E. (1999). *Exile & pride: Disability, queerness, and liberation*. Cambridge: South End Press.

Cochran-Smith, M. (2000). Blind vision: Unlearning racism in teacher education. *Harvard Education Review, 70(2)*, 157–90.

Coles, G. S. (1978). The learning-disabilities test battery: Empirical and social issues. *Harvard Educational Review, 48(3)*, 313–40.

Corbett, J. (1996). *Bad mouthing: The language of special needs*. London: Falmer Press.

Corbett, J., & Slee, R. (2000). An international conversation on inclusive education. In F. Armstrong, D. Armstrong, & L. Barton (Eds.), *Inclusive education: Policy, contexts and comparative perspectives* (pp. 133–146). England: David Fulton Publishers.

Danforth, S. (1997). On what basis hope? Modern progress and postmodern alternatives. *Mental Retardation, 35(2)*, 93–106.

Davis, L. (1997). *The disability studies reader*. New York: Routledge.

Edgerton, R. B. (1967). *The cloak of competence: Stigma in the lives of the mentally retarded*. Berkeley: University of California Press.

Erevelles, N. (2000). Educating unruly bodies: Critical pedagogy, disability studies, and the politics of schooling. *Educational Theory, 50(1)*, 25–47.

Ferguson, P. M., Ferguson, D. L., & Taylor, S. (1992). Interpretivism and disability studies. In P. M. Ferguson, D. L. Ferguson, & S. J. Taylor (Eds.). *Interpreting disability: A qualitative reader*. (pp. 1-11). New York: Teachers College Press.

Francis, L., & Silvers, A. (Eds.). (2000). *Americans with disabilities: Exploring implications of the law for individuals and institutions.* New York: Routledge.

Gabel, S. (2001). Some conceptual problems with critical pedagogy. *Journal of Curriculum Inquiry, 32*(2), 177–202.

Gallagher, D. (1998). The scientific knowledge base of special education: Do we know what we think we know? *Exceptional Children, 64*(4), 493–502.

Golfus, B., & Simpson, D. E. (Producers). (1994). *When Billy broke his head … and other tales of wonder* [Film]. (Available from Fanlight Productions, www.fanlight.com.)

Heshusius, L. (2000, April). Breaking the silence: Disability, education, and critical methods. Paper presented at the meeting of the American Educational Research Association, New Orleans, LA.

———— (1986). Pedagogy, special education, and the lives of young children: A critical and futuristic perspective. *Journal of Education 168(3)*, 25-38.

———— (1982). At the heart of the advocacy dilemma: A mechanistic world view. *Exceptional Children 49*, 6-13.

———— (in press). From creative discontent toward epistemological freedom in special education, reflections on a 25 year journey. In D. Gallagher (Ed).

Hockenberry, J. (1995). *Moving violations.* New York: Hyperion.

Iano, R. (1986). Comments related to Professor Heshusius' application of paradigm change to special education. *Journal of Learning Disabilities, 22(10)*, 416–417.

———— (1990). Special education teachers: Technicians or educators? *Journal of Learning Disabilities, 26*(5), 326–29.

Kingsolver, B. (1990). *The poisonwood Bible.* New York: Harper Collins.

Kittay, E. F. (1998). *Love's labor: Essays on women, equality and dependency.* New York: Routledge.

Kolodny, A. (1998). *Failing the future: A dean looks at higher education.* Durham, NC: Duke University Press.

Lawrence, S., & Tatum, B. (1997). Teachers in transition: The impact of antiracist professional development on classroom practice. *Teachers College Record, 99*, 162–178.

Linton, S. (1998). *Claiming disability: Knowledge and identity.* New York: New York University Press.

Lipsky, D. K., & Gartner, A. (1996). Inclusion, school restructuring, and the remaking of American society. *Harvard Educational Review, 66(4)*, 762–96.

MacIntyre, A. (1999). *Dependent rational animals: Why human beings need virtue.* Berkeley: Open Court.

———— (1981. *After virtue: A study in moral theory.* Notre Dame: University of Notre Dame Press.

Mairs, N. (1996). *Waist-high in the world: A life among the nondisabled.* Boston: Beacon Press.

Mehen, H., Hertweck, A., & Meihls, J. L. (1986). *Handicapping the handicapped: Decision making in students' educational careers.* Stanford, CA: Stanford University Press.

Minow, M. (1990). *Making all the difference: Inclusion, exclusion and American law.* Ithaca: Cornell University Press.

Mitchell, D., Snyder, S., & Ware, L. (2001). *Integrating disability studies into secondary curricula.* Summer Institute proposal to the National Endowment for the Humanities.

Nussbaum, M. (2001). Disabled lives: Who cares? *New York Review of Books,* 34–37.

Oliver, M. (1992). Changing the social relations of research production? *Disability, Handicap & Society,* 7(2), 101–114.

Poplin, M. (1987). Self-imposed blindness: The scientific method in education. *Remedial and Special Education,* 8(6), 31–37.

——— (1988a). The reductionist fallacy in learning disabilities: Replicating the past by reducing the present. *Journal of Learning Disabilities, 21(7),* 389–400.

——— (1988b). Hositic/constructivist principles of the teaching/learning process: Implications for the field of learning disabilities. *Journal of Learning Disabilities, 21(7),* 401–416.

——— (1984). Toward an holistic view of persons with learning disabilities. *Learning Disability Quarterly 7,* 290-94.

Rizvi, F., & Christensen, C. (1996). Introduction. In C. Christensen & F. Rizvi (Eds.), *Disability and the Dilemmas of Education and Justice.* Buckingham: Open University Press.

Sarason, S. (1999). Foreword. In S. J. Taylor, & S. D. Blatt (Eds.), *In search of the promised land: The collected papers of Burton Blatt.* American Association of Mental Retardation.

Silvers, A., Wasserman, D. W., & Mahowald, M. B. (1998). *Disability, difference, discrimination: Perspectives on justice in bioethics and public policy.* New York: Rowman & Littlefield.

Skrtic, T. (1991). *Behind special education: A critical analysis of professioinal culture and school organization.* Denver: Love.

Slee, R. (1997). Imported or important theory? Sociological interrogations of disablement and special education. *British Journal of Sociology of Education, 18(3),* 407–419.

Sleeter, C. (1986). Learning disabilities: The social construction of a special education category. *Exceptional Children, 53,* 46-54.

Snyder, S. L., & Mitchell, D. T. (1996). *Vital signs: Crip culture talks back.* Ann Arbor: Brace Yourselves Production.

Stainback, W., & Stainback, S. (Eds.). (1990). *Controversial issues confronting special education.* Boston: Allyn and Bacon.

Tatum, B. (1992). Talking about race, learning about racism: The application of racial identity development theory in the classroom. *Harvard Educational Review, 62* (1), 1–24.

tenBroek, J. (1966). The right to live in the world: The disabled in the law of torts. *California Law Review, 54,* 841–919.

Tomlinson, S. (1982). *A sociology of special education.* London: Routledge & Keegan Paul.

Ware, L. (2000, April). *A collaborative inquiry on understanding disability in secondary and post-secondary settings.* Research proposal to the National Endowment for the Humanities.

——— (2001a). Writing, identity, and the other: Dare we do disability studies? *Journal of Teacher Education, 52(2),* 107–123.

———— (2001b). Beyond special education: In refusal to limit our own humanity. Manuscript submitted for publication.

———— (2002). A moral conversation on disability: Risking the personal in educational contexts. *Hypatia: A Journal of Feminist Philosophy, 17(3)*, 143–171.

———— (in press). Understanding disability and transforming schools. In T. Booth, K. Nes, & M. Stromstad (Eds.), *Reforming teacher education: The challenge of inclusion.* London: Routledge.

———— (forthcoming). Working past pity: What we make of disability in schools. In J. Allan (Ed.), *Inclusion, participation and democracy: What is the purpose?* Dordrecht, The Netherlands: Kluwer Academic Press.

Ware, L. P., & Cartwright, L. (1999). A post-positivist analysis of Facilitated Communication informed by film, cultural and disability studies. Paper presented at (TASH), Chicago, IL.

Wendell, S. (1996). *The rejected body: Feminist philosophical reflections on disability.* Routledge: New York.

8 Slippery Shibboleths: The Shady Side of Truisms in Special Education

Ellen Brantlinger

A major characteristic of curriculum theorizing is that it is "inherently politi-cal, contested, and in a state of productive flux" (Wright, 2000, p. 4). Even so, some educators' recommendations for curriculum seem fixed for all times and all places. Professional consensus and consistency might be an advan-tage. However, given the diverse and dynamic nature of children, schools, and societies, monolithic ideas about curriculum and pedagogy that become part of the standard grammar of schooling must be scrutinized from the per-spectives of all who are affected. There are many entrenched professional positions regarding education that stand out as problematic when viewed from the position of families whose children are traditionally excluded from the mainstream. Positions, phrases, and practices that are espoused repeat-edly and continuously by some educators reach the status of being shibbo-leths—slippery shibboleths, for that matter.

A shibboleth (defined by the *Webster Desk Dictionary* as 1. a peculiarity of usage and speech that distinguishes a particular class or set of persons. 2. a pet phrase of a group or party, (p. 833) is a password, truism, platitude, pet phrase, or "buzz word" that signifies a meaning shared by members of a group. A shibboleth can refer to—and encompass—policies and practices that a group concurs are beneficial and representative of their viewpoint. Certain shibboleths are commonplace in professional circles. They pop up repeatedly as anchors to truth in journal articles or conference speeches. In early childhood education, developmentally appropriate practice (DAP) is a catchword (that fits the definition of a shibboleth) that has come to character-ize the nature of that field's sense of acceptable pedagogy. It is a sacred motto, which a consensus of the National Association for the Education of Young Children (NAEYC) members have declared to be universally valid and beyond criticism (see Bredekamp & Copple, 1997). However, as Sally Lubeck notes, "There is a tendency to assume that DAP is like a giant mag-net that draws to itself everything that is good and kind and pure" (Lubeck, 1998, p. 300). "Individualized" (direct, one-on-one) instruction is the "apple pie" of special education. Like DAP, its validity as the appropriate instruc-tional approach is taken for granted. For example, in the Council for Excep-tional Children, *Today* newsletter, in an editorial column addressing the

"Problems Special Education Teachers Face," every problem (lack of collaborative planning time, lack of instructional time) listed was framed in "for
one-on-one" or "individualized instruction" p. 5).

The Dominance of Certain Shibboleths/Mindsets

The importance of individualized instruction is assumed by special educators. This fact is illustrated by a course title change in my department. A
course that for three decades bore the title, "Teaching Exceptional Children,"
was changed to "Individualized Instruction in Classrooms." Colleagues who
renamed the course apparently believed that "individualized instruction"
was a suitable title—hence an appropriate generalized instructional approach—for a required course for general education majors who would include students who would be identified as disabled in their future
classrooms. The incentive for the new title perhaps was to diminish or eliminate the course's classification overtones by emphasizing the instructional
practice associated with special education. The decision was made by faculty
members who felt that the other teachers in the department would agree this
was a better title. They were surprised to hear objections. My colleagues are
not alone in assuming that individualized instruction is the fully agreed
upon approach for special education. A perusal of journal articles, newsletter
reports, and textbooks indicates that "individualized instruction" is among
the "special education" techniques judged to be effective for children with
special needs. In *CEC Today*, a newsletter of the major professional organization, the lead article, "Problems Special Education Teachers Face," lists constraints (lack of resources and planning time, overwhelming paperwork) for
implementing *individualized instruction* and report that 81% of special educators spend less than five hours per week in one-on-one instruction ("Problems," 2000). Authors glibly claim that the success of individualized
instruction has been proven by research (see, e.g., Rabren, Darch, & Eaves,
1999). Although McCracken (1999) concurs that direct instruction can have
an immediate positive impact on children's learning (that can be measured
by researchers), she provides an argument that is equivalent to Alfie Kohn's
(1993) conclusion about the extensive use of external rewards in schools:
They do more harm than good in the long run. In spite of cautionary notes,
others assume the efficacy of individualized instruction has stood the test of
empirical scrutiny and its validity as a generalized pedagogical practice is
established and beyond criticism.

Before I address the problematic implications of individualized instruction, it is important to note that even those within the individualized
instruction camp must admit that the ideal of meeting all students' needs

through individualized instruction is rarely accomplished. Special education has been billed as a remedial service that helps deficient students become normal (i.e., achieve at a level commensurate with group norms). Its philosophy has been "meeting diverse needs" (see Henley, Ramsey, & Algozzine, 1999, pp. 39–40). However, as a field experience supervisor who has spent thousands of hours in special education classrooms for more than twenty years, I can attest to the fact that the reality of special education self-contained classrooms is inevitably high teacher-pupil ratios (Russ, Chiang, Rylance, & Bongers, 2001). One-on-one instruction, then, is impossible and "individualized instruction" amounts to differentiated but nevertheless indirect teaching through worksheet packets or personally assigned workbooks and texts (e.g., independent seat work). Other attempts to meet individual needs involve whole or small group instruction. Specialized remedial approaches have been designed and used for certain types of "special needs." However, these methods inevitably are variations of general education pedagogical techniques, and, their popularity waxes and wanes, but it is almost always short-lived. It is more typical for the curriculum in special education classes to be watered- or dummied-down versions of the mainstream curriculum. Resource rooms are "supervised study halls" rather than places for remediation or intensive tutoring. Thus, individualized instruction has been a "theoretical practice" that, due to constraints ("Problems" 2000), except in the most distorted way, rarely has been realized in schools. Hence, even the potentially constructive possibilities of individualized instruction generally have not taken place.

Although individualized instruction rarely is realized, the ideal still dominates the thinking of educators and parents. One reason may be that ideas about the importance of individualized instruction are consistent with commonsense or experience-near theories about learning (Geertz, 1983). It seems logical and reasonable that having an accomplished instructor directly teach an unknown skill, concept, or piece of knowledge would be the most efficient and effective way for a child to learn. Embedded in that judgment is the further assumption that the best way for anyone to learn is to follow the sequential patterns that appear integral to skills and subject area knowledge. In spite of rhetoric about progressive pedagogical approaches, some form of direct instruction of "essential" skills and knowledge is held to be a viable educational practice generally (see Brantlinger & Madj-Jabbari, 1998), and considered a necessity for students with "special needs" (Epps & Tindal, 1987; McDonnell, McLaughlin, & Morrison, 1997; Glatthorn & Craft-Tripp, 2000).

When I contend that individualized instruction is tied to commonsense notions of how people learn, I speak from firsthand experience. In 1963, some years prior to the onslaught of special education pullout programming, I did social studies student teaching in a heterogeneous middle-school classroom. During this teaching, I became concerned about the vast achievement disparities between students. I was distressed about the few who could hardly read, write, and compute. Based on my own ease in learning, I generalized that everybody would have the same success if given a chance; I naively assumed that what is taught is learned. I was convinced that if I could spend more time directly instructing the low achievers, they would become as proficient as their peers. That hunch was why I promptly accepted a special education position when offers for social studies teaching jobs were not forthcoming. Determined to help slow learners "catch up," I was sure I would accomplish that goal in my junior high special education class for students labeled "educable mentally retarded"—those with high-incidence, school-identified "disabilities." At the end of the year, in spite of my conscientious efforts and my pupils' eagerness to learn, to my dismay, few of my eighteen ten- to nineteen-year-old students made substantial progress, and none were up to grade level. Moreover, for the three years I taught in that self-contained class, I was a firsthand witness to the pain and humiliation caused by denigrating labels and their dissatisfaction with being in a special class. By the end of my first year, my dreams about the impact of individualized instruction were tarnished. It might be argued that I had not been able to individualize and directly instruct because of the large pupil-teacher ratio, however, I was hired by some parents to tutor their children before and/or after school on an almost daily basis. These students made slightly more progress, but I found that by the end of a summer without daily practice they returned to school no more advanced than they had been before.

I was an advocate for inclusion, progressive teaching approaches, and constructivist ideas about how children learn. I became convinced that, although a certain amount of individualized instruction can help students overcome misunderstandings and skill and knowledge gaps, it is not appropriate as generalized pedagogy.

Why Slippery?

Philosophers use "slippery slope" for ethical dilemmas in which an idea or a practice seems logical and appropriate, but because of similarity to undesirable practices/ideas or possible negative outcomes, care must be exercised in endorsing it. Philosophers worry that "small beginnings lead to..." or a "foot in the door" will have broader implications than desired and that situations resulting from slippage can get out of hand. In using "slippery" with the individualized instruction "shibboleth," my claim is that, although the concept is perfectly reasonable in many circumstances, its extension to being advocated as the most appropriate way to frame pedagogy particularly for low achievers, is problematic. Similarly, developmentally appropriate practice (DAP), the philosophy that children should be exposed to content or taught in ways compatible with their current levels of achievement, gets slippery when applied mainly to other people's children.

Flawed Assumptions That Underlie DAP and Individualized Instruction

Two aspects of DAP and individualized instruction have potential for damage. One lies with the theories of learning and mental processing that they imply. The other is the nature of practices that inevitably follow from assumptions about their validity.

Progressive education's focus is on discovery learning, independent problem solving, social learning, enriched literacy, and math learning opportunities. Hence, progressive educators emphasize the dynamic complexities of the brain. In contrast, assumptions about the "black box"—behaviorists deliberately chose not to speculate about the mind which they referred to as the "black box"—for individualized instruction advocates seems to be that the mind is like a tape recorder that takes in data one piece at a time and processes new information in a static, incremental way and stores it along with old information just as libraries organized card catalog systems. This linear-processing model of the brain was challenged by Vygotsky and his followers, who inscribe the child as an active, social, culturally contexted constructor of knowledge from multifaceted sources (see Baker, 1999). Even so, in spite of the popularity of constructivist theories at universities and in the professional literature, my own observations in schools indicates that much of education is framed within a subject matter/mental linear developmental model in which learners are to acquire and retain prescribed subject content and literacy skills and demonstrate these on standardized tests. Paulo Freire (1989) calls this the "banking concept" of education, a tradition which, certainly, has dominated traditional special education. *Traditional* here denotes those who believe that deficits (identified as disabilities) are within certain children and that special educators' role is to help children overcome deficits. An "inclusive" educator believes it is normal and acceptable for children to vary and that the teachers' role is to engage and educate all types of children together. Other theories periodically attract notice. However, a perusal of the field's methods and materials indicates that the emphasis has been on getting discrete, measurable chunks of information and skills into learners so they might improve enough to be considered "normal" and "ready" for the mainstream. According to this paradigm, special education is to bring identified students closer to the statistical academic achievement average of chronological age peers—a benchmark thought necessary by those who support inclusion, but only for "children who are *ready* because they are the *same*."

In incorporating pedagogical theories more appropriate for the general education inclusion of diverse children, recent special education textbooks do diverge from the narrow individualized instruction solution by covering cooperative grouping and other techniques suggested by inclusion advocates (for a prime example of creative techniques, see Sapon-Shevin, 1999). Nevertheless, most texts are steeped in an "individualistic model" that "attributes difficulties to *within child* factors associated with medical and charity discourses" (Allan, Brown, & Riddell, 1998, p. 21). Most have not completely abandoned the field's behaviorist origins and leanings. One text includes primarily "drill and practice" software for computer-assisted instruction and carefully lays out plans for direct instruction (Smith, Polloway, Patton, & Dowdy, 2001). Others, although the authors hold divergent views of disabilities and special education (Meyen & Skrtic, 1995, challenge the cascade of services; Hallahan & Kauffman, 2000, defend them), still refer to individualized instruction as a mandated part of the Individualized Educational Plan necessary for all students classified as disabled and suggest using task analysis, teaching by objectives, criterion measures, domain testing, mastery learning, programmed instruction, applied behavioral analysis, curriculum-based assessment, skills-based computer-assisted instruction, frequent feedback, and concrete rewards. In other words, the texts continue to gravitate toward the linear model of children's learning.

A problematic aspect of DAP and individualized instruction approaches is that, even though they are aimed at helping children become similar, paradoxically, both assume definitive and lasting differences among children. As Baker notes: "Developmentalism [the grounding philosophy of both DAP and individualized instruction] drew around the child in terms of inscribing difference and then perceiving it as a problem to be managed"(Baker, 1999, p. 823). Developmental psychology focuses on delineating differences whether they are perceived as temporary delays or permanent distinctions. Lorrie A. Shepard shows how the "Curriculum of Social Efficiency," combined with the "Hereditarian Theory of Intelligence" and "Scientific Measurement," characterize the dominant twentieth-century paradigm ("Role of Assessment," 2000, p. 6). In their 432-page book, *The Nature of Learning Disabilities: Critical Elements of Diagnosis and Classifications,* Kavale and Forness (1995) conclude that LD is a "real phenomenon" and "legitimate special education classification" (p. 333). In comparing American and Japanese early childhood education, Diane M. Hoffman (2000) writes that "the United States has been influenced deeply by notions of developmentally appropriate practice" with "an emphasis on differences across discrete developmental domains, in which the whole child is essentially lost." She further concludes that, in the United States, "child development expertise contributes to an emotional impoverishment in teachers' relations with children as well as to inaccuracies of educators' self-perception in work with children" (p. 193). Differences among students become salient and pivotal; commonalities are either not observed or are considered unimportant.

The Inevitable Destination of the Slippery Slope

Shibboleths are shibboleths precisely because of the prevalence and extensiveness of their shared meanings for groups. Such truisms are integrally related to practice. In the case of the shibboleth of individualized instruction, teachers seek feasible ways to "individualize" for certain children. This approach has tended to involve identifying divergent learners, specifying the nature of their problems, and designing remedies such as the ubiquitous ability groups, tracks, and instruction in such pull-out settings as Title One or special education classrooms. As Hoffman (2000) observes: "In the United States, the focus on individual differences results in highly differentiated curricular experiences across assumed levels of ability" (p. 196). Perhaps nobody intends to segregate students. Even so, it follows from the assumptions that individualized instruction is an effective strategy for low achievers, and separated settings are conducive to direct instruction. This conduciveness is slippery. While not deliberately advocating segregation, it has happened in the past and will probably always happen if educators buy into the shibboleth, individualized instruction.

One of the most troubling aspects of special education is that among children classified as disabled and educated in restrictive placements (i.e., segregated from peers; little access to the general curriculum), there has been a persistent pattern of overrepresentation of children who are poor or from historically marginalized groups. Special education is not unique in this regard. All low-status arrangements (vocational education, low tracks, compensatory programs) are subject to the same phenomenon, while poor children and children of color are underrepresented in high status gifted and talented programs, advanced tracks, competitive and prestigious extracurricular activities. A few decades ago, disparaging classifications were doled out loosely. Modern special education has become legalized (infused with the language of equal protection and due process) and scientific (based on statistically normed, objective-seeming measures), so that both providers and recipients of services are easily convinced that the system is fair and legitimate. Nevertheless, cavalier labeling continues. "At risk," another derogatory label, is used in an indiscriminate and overgeneralized way. Indeed, risk is synonymous with low-income or minority status.

Both DAP and individualized instruction have had profound implications for determining appropriate placement and shaping services for students identified as having disabilities or being "at risk." Adherents of DAP emphasize the importance of learning through play and tend to disparage direct instruction (Charlesworth, 1998). However, their thinking converges with individualized instruction advocates in their response to diversity. Goals for children and, subsequently, pedagogy and curriculum, vary according to beliefs about children's achievement (Wright, Diener, & Kay, 2000). Professionals feel that certain learners are not ready for the same advanced curriculum and activities as their peers. Difference becomes the rationale for segregation and unique curricula, which is pernicious because it relegates other people's children to a lesser status and diminished circumstance. Head Start, designed for preschool children from low-income families, often has a social skills and "let them play" emphasis, whereas private community preschools that cater to wealthier children push intellectual enrichment and academic acceleration. My own observations of the social skills emphasis of Head Start programs are confirmed by those of Inoway-Ronnie (1998). For early childhood educators DAP means to delay introducing an advanced curriculum for "less ready" learners; for special educators the solution is to differentiate instruction and have it take place in settings where the curriculum is watered- or dummied-down.

Then, when the achievement gap widens, rather than acknowledge the effects of disparate curriculum, the discrepancy becomes evidence that "early intervention" is not effective enough to reverse "social and cultural deficits." Other factors that enter into this achievement discrepancy equation are ignored. It is rarely mentioned that schools in impoverished urban and rural areas are substantially underfunded and decelerated in comparison to the suburban schools (Kozol, 1991). The next step is for certain scholars to see achievement disparities as evidence of racial and class distinctions in inherited intelligence (Herrnstein & Murray, 1994). Based on the ambiguous coverage of the Bell Curve in the popular press, it seems that such attitudes are prevalent among the general public. Achievement, then, translates into personal worth, so when students leave school huge wage differentials appear justified. The rich stay rich and the poor stay poor. The gap between the salaries and assets of people widens.

What comes first in this damaging cycle is irrelevant. From an educational perspective, what is important is that shibboleths give credence to discriminatory practice. So, the slippery aspect of the shibboleths individualized instruction and DAP is that they apply to children who are the most vulnerable and whose parents have little power to control their children's educational circumstances. It is not that falling behind or needing individualized instruction does not occur among middle-class children. However, in their case, individualized instruction is selected as a partial and/or temporary technique to supplement but not replace general school participation. It occurs to help them overcome difficulties or improve their performance, but rarely results in permanent educational placements. Conversely, DAP is the rationale that justifies such advantaged placements as gifted and talented, honor, or advanced placement programs.

My work documents the salience of class biases and subsequent school advantages for the children of supposedly liberal professional parents (Brantlinger, Madj-Jabbari, & Guskin, 1996), as well as how negative social class images are internalized by low-income parents (Brantlinger, 1985). Rosenthal and Jacobson's (1968) dramatic study raised awareness of self-fulfilling prophecies. My interviews with high- and low-income adolescents also indicate that class stereotypes undergird their thinking and affect how they perceive the educational needs of students from different classes (Brantlinger, 1993).

Does the Mandated Individual Education Plan Necessitate Individualized Instruction?

Federal legislation mandates attention to, and documentation of, all classified students' special needs through the vehicle of an Individualized Education Plan/Program. However, this personal attention mandate does not require any particular instructional arrangement. Certainly, a range of curricula and instructional techniques are appropriate for classified children. Nevertheless, the *modus operandi* for special education is basic skill instruction. Indeed, the lower the measured skills of students, the more likely they are to have a narrow skills-based curriculum. Again, this skills-repetition and curriculum reduction is not unique to special education. The same is true of instruction in low tracks and high-poverty schools. In schools with low scores on high-stakes testing, teachers often are required to teach specific facts in a linear fashion for months prior to the period when tests are given. Indeed, the whole curriculum may be built around the content expected on tests—tedious and dull routines, again, demanded for the students who most need their curriculum to be intrinsically interesting and exciting because the extrinsic carrot of learning to prepare for college is not part of their lives.

What Does DAP and Individualized Instruction Mean to Its Recipients?

Although there are few emic studies of what it means to be called disabled, anyone who has spent much time around classified students can testify that disability labels are resented. Students who receive services are less likely to evaluate them as helpful and necessary than students with no experience with special education and little likelihood of being placed there (Brantlinger, 1994). Consumers of other second-class services also do not endorse them. Wrigley writes that working class parents preferred comprehensive to vocational schools for their offspring and are not in favor of compensatory educational arrangements (Wrigley, 1982). In some countries vocational education may be valued because it includes instruction of useful skills for attaining a job and because working-class jobs pay enough for a decent lifestyle. In the United States, with few resources going to high-powered programs and with such a low wage structure for working-class jobs, vocational education is unlikely to be highly regarded or seen as equivalent to a comprehensive high school or college preparatory curriculum. Regarding endorsement of Head Start by working classes, in Milwaukee, the local Congress on Racial Equality (CORE) chapter criticized the segregation of Head Start facilities and threatened to boycott them if the programs did not eliminate racial segregation (Kuntz, 1998). Of course, Head Start is class segregated by design. In the early 1980s, low-income parents told me that they preferred class-heterogeneous schools for their children (Brantlinger, 1985). A New Zealand study of school choice found that low-income parents had the same values and judgments about their school preferences for their children as high-income parents, yet circumstances having to do with lower incomes prevented them from the breadth of school selections that were realized by their more affluent counterparts (Lauder et al., 1999). Using national survey data of 12,500 high school students to examine the impact of algebra on students who differ in their math skills prior to entering high school, Pallas found that all benefit from taking algebra. Replicating results of earlier research in other countries, a New Zealand study found that school effectiveness for low-income students rests upon the presence and cultural resources of students from middle-class families (Thrupp, 1998). In the UK, despite convincing research evidence of the benefits of heterogeneous classrooms, Reay found that administrators segregated by "ability" not as a result of convictions about "best practice," but because of pressures for examination success rates and middle-class parental preference (Reay, 1998). Asserting that the "progress throughout the western world was free and equal state-provided education," which "promoted both social cohesion and mobility," Sirkka (2000) claims that as "neo-liberal economics takes over policy discourse, school systems are converted into marketplaces, which create or exacerbate socioeconomic segregation" (p. 483), but "educational achievement tends to be higher in countries with strong state regulation of schooling" (pp. 488, 490).

Educational camps interpret the well-documented social class correlation with school achievement and attainment differently. Social Darwinists attribute class distinctions to the genetic heritage of children. Critical theorists see discrimination in society and especially in such social institutions as schools. In this chapter, I have tried to illustrate that shibboleths that revolve around developmental philosophies are vehicles for sanctioning differential treatment of children from different classes. The trouble is that these shibboleths are so ingrained in our thinking and so embedded in a complex of related ideologies about schooling and life that they are hard to discern for what they are and what they do. It is difficult to recognize how we professionals, as class-positioned subjects, benefit from such shibboleths. Williams explains that hegemony refers to the "rationalization of relations of domination and subordination, in their forms as practical consciousness," so that they are the "limits of simple experience and common sense" (Williams, 1989, p. 57).

Baker criticizes those of us who "strategize to destabilize developmentalism in relation to power, the subject, and timespace" because of its danger regarding diverse humans, yet still leave modernist narratives of human freedom in place (1999, pp. 825, 826, 827, 828). Baker turns to Walkerdine (1993), who argues that one cannot stay inside logocentric and western conceptions of rationality and still deconstruct developmentalism; it is rationality that provides the grounds for marginalizing others. Some (e.g., Apffel-Marlin & Marglin, 1996) maintain that if we listen to non-western people who do not separate generative activities from cultural activities, we can learn nonmodernist ways of being in the world and learn to see "modern knowledge" as a form of local knowledge. Such new epistemologies are necessary if women and men from different class, ethnic, and cultural positions are to engage in collective emancipatory projects without reproducing patterns of hierarchy and domination. Drawing from Sandra Harding, Bailey defines "traitorous subjects" as those who belong to dominant groups yet resist the usual assumptions and practices of those groups; that is, they are "privilege-cognizant" rather than "privilege-evasive" as they "refuse to animate expected whitely scripts and are unfaithful to worldviews whites are expected to hold" (Bailey, 2000, p. 283). Agreeing with Maria Lugones (1987),

Bailey suggests we "world travel" to get out of locations and texts in which we feel at home, develop new habits, and let our identities fall apart (Bailey, 2000, p. 296). Extending developmentalist thinking to a global perspective, Barker contends, "The language of development is a discourse infused with the Enlightenment ideal of innocent knowledge that masks the instrumental role that development has played in maintaining global structures of neocolonialism and dependency. Missing from this analysis is awareness of the role that development rhetoric and policies played in producing underdevelopment, exploitation, and oppression" (Barker, 2000, p. 177).

Curricular Determinates: What Is Education For? (What Is Life For?)

An observation based on my interaction with my parents in their old age and through reading mature authors (see Martin, 2000; Rorty, 1998) is that they begin to ask deep, comprehensive questions about life. As my mother broke up the family home, she not only puzzled about what to do with the objects she had acquired through the years, she pondered why they had seemed important. Rather than dwelling on my educational and occupational achievement as she had in earlier years, she worried about my proximity to her. As we struggle to compete with peers and colleagues in various social settings throughout our lives, we fail to see our place in broader human and nonhuman environments. When we look at development's ebb and flow over a lifetime, the fine distinctions in rates of human learning that were observed tend to dissipate and disappear. Oh, that we could reach that wisdom at an earlier age.

References

Allan, J., Brown, S., & Riddell, S. (1998). Permission to speak? Theorizing special education inside the classroom. In C. Clark, A.Dyson, & A. Millward (Eds.), *Theorising special education* (pp. 21–31). London: Routledge.

Apffel-Marlin, F., & Marglin, S. A. (1996). (Eds.). *Decolonizing knowledge: From development to dialogue*. Oxford: Clarendon Press.

Bailey, A. (2000). Locating traitorous identities: Toward a view of privilege-cognizant white character. In U. Narayan & S. Harding (Eds.), *Decentering the center: Philosophy for a multicultural, postcolonial, and feminist world* (pp. 283–298). Bloomington: Indiana University Press.

Baker, B. (1999, winter). The dangerous and the good? Developmentalism, progress, and public schooling. *American Educational Research Journal, 36*, 797–834.

Barker, D. (2000). Dualisms, discourse, and development. In U. Narayan & S. Harding (Eds.), *Decentering the center: Philosophy for a multicultural, postcolonial, and feminist world* (pp. 177–188). Bloomington: Indiana University Press.

Brantlinger, E. (1985). Low-income parents' opinions about the social class composition of schools. *American Journal of Education, 93*, 389–408.

———— (1993). *The politics of social class in secondary schools: Views of affluent and impov-erished youth.* New York: Teachers College Press.

———— (1994). High-income and low-income adolescents' views of special education. *Journal of Adolescent Research, 9(3),* 384–407.

Brantlinger, E., & Madj-Jabbari, M. (1998). The conflicted pedagogical and curricular perspectives of middle-class mothers. *Journal of Curriculum Studies,* 30(4), 431–460.

Brantlinger, E., Madj-Jabbari, M., & Guskin, S. L. (1996, fall). Self-interest and liberal Educational discourse: How ideology works for middle-class mothers. *American Educational Research Journal, 33,* 571–598.

Bredekamp, S., & Copple, C. (Eds.). (1997). *Developmentally appropriate practice in early childhood programs.* Washington, DC: National Association for the Education of Young Children.

Charlesworth, R. (1998). Response to Sally Lubeck's "Is developmentally appropriate practice for everyone?" *Childhood Education, 74(5),* 293–298.

Editors, (2000, November). Problems special education teachers face. *CEC Today, Vol. 9,* 1–16.

Epps, S., & Tindal, G. (1987). The effectiveness of differential programming in serving students with mild handicaps. In M. C. Wang, M. C. Reynolds, & H. J. Walberg (Eds.), *Handbook of special education: Research and practice. Vol. 1* (pp. 213–250). New York: Pergamon.

Freire, P. (1989). *Pedagogy of the oppressed.* New York: Continuum, 1989.

Geertz, C. (1983). *Local knowledge: Further essays in interpretive anthropology.* New York: Basic Books.

Glatthorn, A. A., & Craft-Tripp, M. (2000). *Standards-based learning for students with disabilities.* Larchmont, NY: Eye on Education.

Hallahan, D. P., & Kauffman, J. (2000). *Exceptional Learners: Introduction to Special Education* (8th ed.). Boston: Allyn & Bacon.

Henley, M., Ramsey, R. S., & Algozzine, R. (1999). *Teaching students with mild disabilities* (3rd ed.). Boston: Allyn & Bacon.

Herrnstein, R., & Murray, C. (1994). *The bell curve: The reshaping of American live by differences in intelligence.* New York: Free Press.

Hoffman, D. (2000). Pedagogies of self in American and Japanese early childhood education: Critical conceptual analysis. *Elementary School Journal, 101,* 193–208.

Inoway-Ronnie, E. (1998). High/scope in Head Start programs serving Southeast Asian immigrant and refugee children and their families: Lessons from an ethnographic study. In J. Ellsworth & L. J. Ames (Eds.), *Critical perspectives on project Head Start: Revisioning the hope and challenge* (pp. 167–199). Albany: State University of New York Press.

Kavale, K. A., & Forness, S. R. (1995). *The nature of learning disabilities: Critical elements of diagnosis and classifications.* Mahwah, NJ: Lawrence Erlbaum.

Kohn, A. (1993). *Punished by rewards: The trouble with gold stars, incentive plans, A's, praise, and other bribes.* Boston: Houghton Mifflin.

Kozol, J. (1991). *Savage inequalities: Children in America's schools.* New York: HarperPerennial.

Kuntz, K. R. (1998). A lost legacy: Head start's origins in community action. In I. Ellsworth & L. J. Ames (Eds.), *Critical perspectives on project Head Start: Revisioning the hope and challenges* (pp. 1-48). Albany: State Univerity of New York Press.

Lauder, H., Hughes, D., Watson, S. Waslander, S., Thrupp, M., Strathdee, R., Simiyu, I., Dupuis, A., McGlinn, J., & Hamlin J. E. (1999). *Trading in futures: Why markets in education don't work.* Buckingham, UK: Open University Press.

Lubeck, S. (1998). Is DAO for everyone? A response. *Childhood Education, 74(5),* 299–301.

Lugones, M. (1987). Playfulness, world-travelling, and loving perception. *Hypatia, 2(2),* 3–19.

Martin, J. R. (2000). *Coming of age in academe: Rekindling women's hopes and reforming the academy.* New York: Routledge.

McCracken, J. B. (1999). Professional books. *Childhood Education, 74,* 314–317.

McDonnell, L. M., McLaughlin, M. J., & Morrison, P. M. (1997). *Educating one and all.* Washington, DC: National Academy Press.

Meyen, E. L., & Skrtic, T. M. (1995). (Eds.). *Special education and student disability* (4th ed.). Denver, CO: Love Publishing Company

Rabren, K., Darch, C., & Eaves, R. (1999). The differential effects of two systematic reading comprehension approaches with students with learning disabilities. *Journal of Learning Disabilities, 32(1),* 36–47.

Reay, D. (1998). Setting the agenda: The growing impact of market forces on pupil grouping in British secondary schooling. *Journal of Curriculum Studies 30(5),* 545–558.

Role of assessment in a learning culture. (2000, October). *Educational Researcher, 29(7),* 4–14.

Rorty, R. (1998). *Achieving our country: Leftist thought in twentieth-century America.* Cambridge, MA: Harvard University Press.

Rosenthal, R., & Jacobson, L. (1968). *Pygmalion in the classroom.* New York: Holt, Rinehart and Winston.

Sirkka, A. (2000). What happens to the common school in the market? *Journal of Curriculum Studies, 32(4),* 483–493.

Russ, S., Chiang, B., Rylance, B. J., & Bongers, J. (2001). Caseload in special education: An integration of research findings. *Exceptional Children, 67(2),* 161–172.

Sapon-Shevin, M. (1999). *Because we can change the world: A practical guide to building cooperative, inclusion classroom communities.* Needham Heights, MA: Allyn & Bacon.

Smith, T. E., Polloway, E. A., Patton, J. R., & Dowdy, C. A. (2001). *Teaching students with special needs in inclusive settings* (3rd ed.). Boston: Allyn & Bacon.

Thrupp, M. (1998). The art of the possible: Organizing and managing high and low socio-economic schools. *Journal of Education Policy, 13(2),* 197–219.

Walkerdine, V. (1993). Beyond developmentalism? *Theory and Psychology, 3,* 451–469.

Webster desk dictionary. (1983). New York: Gamercy Books.

Williams, R. (1989). Hegemony and the selective tradition. In S. de Castell, A. Luke, and C. Luke (Eds.), *Language, authority and criticism: Readings on the school textbook* (pp. 56–60). Lewes: Falmer.

Wright, C., Diener, M., & Kay, S. C. (2000). School readiness of low-income children at risk for school failure. *Journal of Children & Poverty, 6(2),* 99–117.

Wright, H. K. (2000). Nailing jell-o to the wall: Pinpointing aspects of state-of-the-art curriculum theorizing. *Educational Researcher, 29,* 4–13.

Wrigley, J. (1982). *Class politics and public schools: Chicago 1900–1950.* New Brunswick, NJ: Rutgers University Press.

9 Searching for Something Outside of Ourselves: The Contradiction Between Technical Rationality and the Achievement of Inclusive Pedagogy

Deborah J. Gallagher

> I have spent my entire career searching for the next curricular program or set of materials that would get my students to achieve their prescribed learning objectives. Somehow, I believed that just around the corner I would find the right techniques, the right methods, that would work. I just never believed that teaching my students came from inside of me.
>
> (Student in a Graduate Education Seminar)

These are the words spoken by an experienced teacher during a graduate seminar on critical issues in education. The topic of discussion centered on the question of how to teach diverse learners in inclusive educational environments. This teacher's comment illustrates, at least up to that moment of realization, how many educators have come to conceptualize their work largely as a technical undertaking requiring the application of standard curricula through prescribed pedagogical methods. It reveals a mind-set deeply situated in the search for an objective external authority in which to ground the teaching/learning process, a seeking for something outside of oneself to which individual educators can demonstrate professional accountability.

Although the infusion of objectivist technical-rationality into all facets of schooling has long been subject to serious critique (Callahan, 1962; Hodkinson, 1997; Skrtic, 1991a, 1991b), its widespread appeal to a sizable portion of education professionals, policy makers, and the public has ensured its enduring influence. The result has been an impetus toward an increasing emphasis on measurable "basic skills" instruction, lockstep curricula with accompanying basal textbook adoption, and pedagogical procedures that have gone from the merely prescriptive to the literally scripted (e.g., the "SRA Direct Instruction Programs" and the "Success for All" program). This is especially the case with students who constitute the ranks of the lowest achieving students such as those in special education or "at-risk" programs, and reflects the logic that they need more of what is good for all students.

In turn, this "more of the same" logic suggests to many that low-achieving students require separate placements if they are to benefit from this form of intensive instruction, i.e., if they are going to get the help they need to remedy their problems. From this point of view, segregated placements are justified, if not on the basis of their desirability, then certainly on the basis of their inevitability (Kauffman, 1995; MacMillan, Gresham, & Forness, 1996). However, as the debate over inclusion clearly illustrates, a growing number of educators, as well as parents and other advocates, find this acceptance of the inevitable to be decidedly unacceptable. Citing the inherent inequality of segregated placements, inclusion advocates have made progress toward raising inclusive education as a worthy goal. Moreover in many schools, a measure of success toward inclusion has been achieved.

That notwithstanding, the professional literature is replete with seemingly intractable obstacles to inclusion. For example, scholars have frequently cited that general education teachers are inadequately "trained" to teach special needs students, that these students cannot keep up and are doomed to failure, and that students who are physically included in the general classroom are not included in educationally or socially meaningful ways (Kavale, 2000). Perhaps the most crucial, but rarely mentioned, obstacle is that educators have been trying to get the technical-rational approach, the very one that contributed to the segregation of special education students, to now work in getting them back into the general education classroom. In this chapter, I contend that because many general education classrooms are rooted in this conceptual framework, any meaningful efforts toward genuine inclusion must therefore begin at this juncture.

In the following portions of this chapter, I start by tracing the historical influences of the technical-rational mind-set to demonstrate how educators have come to look outside of themselves to define the nature of their work. I then define, describe, and characterize a constructivist alternative and discuss how educators might begin moving toward this alternative.

Tracing the Historical Influences

How do teaching and learning came to be understood as a technical/rational undertaking? The origins of this framework can be traced to the Enlightenment, an intellectual and political movement that embraced science as a means for purging society of the oppressions of religious dogma and authority (Robinson, 1981). Time and space does not allow for a detailed recounting of how Enlightenment thinking led to how we have come to see the world, and our relationship to it, in terms of a mind versus matter dualism. This history has been written elsewhere (see Robinson, 1981; Smith, 1989), but the pivotal point, as advanced by Locke and announced by Compte and Mill in the social sciences, was that a separate reality exists outside of the human mind, and the work of science is to gain knowledge of that independently existing reality. Clearly, from this perspective, we live in a world of facts separated from values, and one in which the social can thus be made amenable to precise intervention once the facts are known. At the core of this undertaking was the appropriation of the scientific method as a tool to eliminate uncertainty by discovering the regularities of the objective world. Simply stated, the reasoning here is—if I can predict the outcome of my own and others' actions, what is uncertain anymore?

Our main focus at this point must be to examine the legacy of this history, and most particularly how its ideas shaped educational discourse and practice. When the scientific method was embraced by empiricist educational researchers, as it was across the social sciences as a whole, most believed that it would offer the same successes it brought to the physical sciences (Giddens, 1993). This approach seemed reasonable enough, given the celebrated accomplishments accrued by the physical sciences through the use of experimental procedures. Educational researchers were understandably exhilarated by the prospect of developing a science of teaching and learning that would allow educators to bring instrumental reasoning and means/ends efficiency to bear on the educational enterprise. The palpable enthusiasm for this project was recorded in the words of educational psychologist, Edward Thorndike, who, in the first edition of *The Journal of Educational Psychology* wrote:

> A complete science of psychology would tell every fact about everyone's intellect and character and behavior, would tell the cause of every change in human nature, would tell the result which every educational force—every act of every person that changed any other or the agent himself—would have. It would aid us to use human beings for the world's welfare with the same surety of the result that we now have when we use falling bodies or chemical elements. In proportion as we get such a science we shall become masters of our own souls as we are now master of heat and light. Progress toward such a science is being made. (Thorndike, 1910, p. 6)

Here, at last, was a means for coping with the uncertainties of teaching, a system for developing a scientifically based set of techniques which would make the process more efficient by boiling it down to the application of effective procedures. More importantly, it would place the burden of judgment outside of ourselves. Much to our detriment that is exactly what has happened.

To accomplish the goal of Thorndike and like-minded others, though, means that educators must deal with facts, eliminate values, get rid of all subjective meaning. In the technical-rational approach to education, ideas and people must be treated like things, and, "... people can be managed as if they behaved like parts of a machine" (Hodkinson, 1997, p. 73); otherwise, it would not work. Watson, and his protégé, Skinner, carried this project even further with their theory of behaviorism, which found its way into classrooms during the last half of the twentieth century and continues to exercise a tenacious hold, particularly in instruction for remedial and special education students. Watson's cardinal premise was that the study of psychology, "must discard all reference to consciousness..." (1913, p. 163). To him, the notion that human beings' search for meaning was an anathema to the study of psychology, thwarting the field's rightful destiny as, "a purely experimental branch of natural science," whose theoretical goal was to be "the prediction and control of behavior" (p. 158). Because human consciousness cannot be tangibly observed, it cannot be verified scientifically; and, if it cannot be verified, it simply does not exist. The inevitable solution to the vexatious problem of consciousness was simply to dispense with it as a fiction, along with the belief in personhood or moral autonomy altogether.

In turn, this bluntly practical resolution gave rise to futuristic scenarios reminiscent of Thorndike's grandiose world of scientific possibility. In what may now strike present-day educators as chillingly repressive, Watson (1924) issued the following challenge that may remind readers of the popular movie "The Truman Show:" "Give me a dozen healthy infants, well-formed, and my own specified world to bring them up in and I'll guarantee to take any one at random and train him to become any type of specialist I might select" (p. 82). Similarly, Skinner, who built a glass, climate-controlled box for his infant daughter (see Cleverley & Phillips, 1986), thoroughly repudiated the belief in consciousness to the extent of starkly denying the entire concept of personhood. This repudiation is captured quite explicitly in the third volume of his autobiography in which he stated, "If I am right about human behavior, I have written the autobiography of a nonperson" (Skinner, 1983, p. 412). Aside from the disturbing incoherency of such an assertion, the upshot of the whole enterprise obviated any considerations of personal or moral agency. From the behaviorists' perspective, human learning is a product of antecedents and consequences, and nothing more.

Although current educators of the traditional behaviorist/empiricist persuasion are as likely as any others to find this position to be decidedly disagreeable, its historical legacy cannot in any case be ignored or denied. As the following analysis demonstrates, the Enlightenment's contribution to the empiricist assumption of subject versus object dualism (along with the behaviorist premise of consciousness as a fabrication) has exercised definitive influence in the technical-rationality of contemporary schooling. In the midst of this analysis, it becomes clear that the technical-rational framework has built into it a number of inevitable contradictions; and, because of the self-synchronizing nature of its assumptions, creates an endless cycle of problems, technical-rational solutions, and the subsequent re-creation of even more complex problems. Once caught in the web of technical-rationality, it is seemingly impossible to escape.

Technical Rationality and the Deskilling of Teachers

A neutral/objective framework, once embraced, invariably leads to teaching that is largely a matter of applying a prescriptive method. Thus, instruction emphasizes form over function and meaning. Teaching mathematics, for example, centers on accurate computation largely devoid of conceptual development; written expression becomes a matter of mastery of mechanics detached from students' authentic writing, and history is reduced to decontextualized rote memorization of names, dates, and discrete events. Accordingly, teachers are led to focus so heavily on the "how-to" demands of instruction that they lose sight of the "whys" of learning.

In effect, technical-rationality drives what Apple (1982) referred to as teacher deskilling, a term that, despite its connotation, does not mean that teachers become less skilled. More to the point, it means that teachers come to abandon any conviction that teaching is about meaning-making. In the process, they literally learn, or better said, are "trained" not to think. The acquisition of more and more teaching techniques, or "skill diversification," as Apple (1993) clarified, embodies the Enlightenment contradiction in that it represents an "intellectual deskilling in which mental workers are cut off from their own fields and again must rely even more heavily on ideas and processes provided by 'experts'" (p. 262). Put differently, teachers learn to search outside of themselves to define the very nature of their work.

I personally witnessed a rather glaring example of this detachment process while observing a student teacher teaching a popular and thoroughly researched strategy for identifying unknown reading vocabulary. As she instructed the three sixth-grade students on the steps for implementing the strategy, they read passages from the classic children's book *Roll of Thunder, Hear My Cry*. Each time they encountered an unfamiliar word, the student teacher reviewed the strategy steps, student memorization of which constituted the behavioral objective of her lesson plan. As events progressed, the students dutifully recited and performed the steps. However, it became increasingly evident from their occasional comments and questions that they were becoming captivated by the rich expression and thematic depth of the novel. Over time, these comments and questions began to diminish as mastering the strategy steps continued throughout to be the focal point of the lesson.

During the subsequent debriefing, the student teacher initially expressed her sense that the lesson had been a success. From her point of view, this was so because she had faithfully executed the steps of the "direct instruction" lesson plan. Toward the conclusion of this discussion, however, she began to disclose, rather tentatively, some lurking doubts. "There were a lot of things I would like to have done," she began. She then elaborated that she would rather have discussed the story in more depth and went on to describe with great enthusiasm the kinds of questions and insights about the novel she would have shared with the students. When asked why she chose not to do so, she replied hesitantly, "Well, I couldn't get that to fit the steps of the direct instruction lesson plan format." She finally added that she did not think that the students would really choose to use the strategy on their own because she could not imagine using it herself in her own personal reading.

Clearly, this student teacher was already well on her way to believing that techniques and procedures should take precedence over meaning and that her own sense of what it means to be a teacher was neither legitimate nor trustworthy. That instrumental reasoning essentially debilitates teachers by stripping them of their role as autonomous intellectual professionals and is revealed in her alienating sense of self-betrayal and diminished confidence.

One other point is in order regarding the above. Because the student teacher was working with special education students, one might argue that the example does not apply to general education classrooms. I would contend that although technical-rationality asserts a stronger influence over special education given its traditions in the medical model, general education is also highly influenced by this same conceptual framework. Many general education teacher preparation programs continue to be informed by this framework. The widespread use of the Madeline Hunter (1986) lesson plan model comes immediately to mind. Perhaps more importantly, teachers from more progressive preparation programs go on to teach in schools that require adherence to basal textbook programs and, more recently, curriculums heavily driven by standardized test preparation materials. Further, given the current political emphasis on "evidence-based practices" written into the federal "No Child Left Behind" legislation, general education has come under increasing pressure to embrace the technical-rational framework of teaching.

In the following excerpt, Heshusius (1984) has expressed rather poignantly the desperation and alienation technical rationality inspires in teachers:

> I remember looking at the drawers full of programmed materials, worksheets, task-analyzed tasks, phonic exercises, remedial programs, all showing a remarkable similarity: pieces of things. Filling in blanks. Filling in letters. Word-attack skills for isolated words. Marking multiple choice answers. I would force myself to read it all, or rather not to read but to skim, for there was nothing to really read. I would get lost, then force myself to start over again, and I would invariably feel a tiredness, a sudden fatigue. I was not absorbing anything. My own mind had become a blank. Yet, I would tell myself: I need to use them, for weren't others doing so, and didn't all these publishers publish them, didn't theories support them, didn't I see them in curriculum laboratories and at instructional materials exhibitions? I would think of the students I had to teach the next day, and I would feel depressed, powerless, even desperate. For why would they want to learn something that was boring, that could not even hold one minute of my own interest, that made no sense contextually, that contained nothing a person wanted to learn? (p. 364)

Under these circumstances, one might then question whether the technical-rational thrust empowers or debilitates teachers. Moreover, when teachers are literally "trained" not to make sense of their own teaching, is it any wonder that students have difficulty making sense of learning?

Technical Rationality and the Disabling of Students

Not unlike their teachers, students are also "de-skilled." Because tightly controlled, unidirectional teaching leaves the learner passive (Poplin, 1988), "traits" such as inattentiveness, memory "deficits," and low motivation become more evident in a portion of students. Heshusius (1984) proposed that these traits have more to do with sheer boredom and detachment than with the presumed intrinsic qualities of the learner. This idea applies, by the way, not only to those who are labeled as having mild disabilities. Those with what are termed moderate and severe disabilities are similarly affected, as are those who are viewed as average and even high-achieving students. This does not mean that elimination of technical-rationality will result in all students learning in a uniform fashion, which of course constitutes another misguided dimension of the drive to segregate. However, what it does suggest is that many of the learning problems of students who are eventually referred to special education are instigated and exacerbated by technical/rational teaching practices (Iano, 2003). In effect, we create the learning problems we later seek to eliminate, with subsequent solutions creating even more complex problems, and so on (Gallagher, 1998).

The question that might be raised here is—if all students are poorly affected by the technical rationality of schools, why is it more problematic for some students than others? There are numerous explanations, all of which are distinctly related to the technical/rational framework under which schools predominantly operate. These include the fundamental conceptual flaws of the normative mind-set (Hacking, 1990; MacKenzie, 1981) (particularly as manifested in educational assessment practices), the ideology of capitalist competition (Bowles & Gintis, 1976; Boyles, 1998), and the politically driven insistence that schools serve as sorting and selecting mechanisms (Chapman, 1988; Spring, 1989). With regard to the technical conception of teaching, several scholars have pointed out that students from culturally or ethnically diverse backgrounds, as well as those from impoverished backgrounds, lead lives that differ in so many facets that school tasks and activities are at tremendous odds with much of what is meaningful, and therefore accessible, to them (Dudley-Marling, 1996; Iano, 1990). "Thus, the technical framework and its decontextualization and neutralization of skills, along with the devaluation of minority and lower class cultures, can often serve to undermine education, teaching, and learning" (Iano, 1990, p. 464). Should we be surprised by the seemingly intractable overrepresentation of culturally diverse and lower-income students in special needs programs?

Conversely, students whose home backgrounds represent the dominant culture come to school with sufficient "cultural capital" (Bourdieu & Passeron, 1977) in terms of language, values, and experience that they are able to override, so to speak, the constricting effects of this framework. To reiterate, this does not mean that they are not adversely affected, but rather are able to perform in ways that have all the appearances of surviving, or even thriving. Interestingly, some have suggested that those who are not surviving actually serve to reveal the flaws and limitations of the current system that affect all students (Sapon-Shevin, 1996; Singham, 1998). A very good case can be made that seeking an alternative inclusive pedagogy will benefit all students, not just those students who experience its most obvious and incapacitating effects.

A Constructivist Approach to Inclusive Pedagogy

In contrast to this technical-rational mind-set, it is vital to propose a constructivist alternative if we are to achieve truly inclusive schooling. Toward that end, I describe or characterize the constructivist framework. This is no small task, for a number of reasons. First, constructivism is not a theory of teaching, per se. Instead, it is a theory of knowledge, or epistemology, which forms a conceptual basis for teaching practices that are consistent with its philosophical tenants. Because it is an emerging paradigm, one will find variation in how constructivist principles are interpreted and enacted. As Poplin (1988) observed, constructivism is only one of several terms used to describe this emerging paradigm, all of which share in common, but are not entirely defined by, an opposition to reductionistic, technical, or mechanistic ways of teaching and learning. Among these terms, she cited Piaget's (1970) structuralism, "a philosophic method for collecting, perceiving, organizing, and interpreting phenomena," and Bronfenbrenner's (1979) holism, which recognizes "other, noncognitive, variables related to learning, such as those generally related with feelings or intuitive thought, motivation, and larger sociological variables" (p. 402). What some educators may also find confusing is a multitude of other terms associated with constructivism, such as *whole language, progressive education, humanistic, learner-centered approaches,* and *hands-on* or *discovery teaching* methods.

A second and further complication is that very often these terms (especially the latter ones) find their way into practice devoid of, or abstracted from, any coherent understanding of their conceptual moorings. In these instances, teaching practices claiming these banners devolve into something of a "cookbook approach" reminiscent of the technical-rational framework (Brooks & Brooks, 1993). In effect, the terms are co-opted in a misguided, though sincere, attempt to locate a compromise or reconciliation between the two incommensurate frameworks. Absent a deeply informed grasp of the underlying principles, and in the presence of the often contentious discourse between advocates of these opposing frameworks, it is more than understandable how educators might wish to find a means for incorporating what, in their view, might be the "best of both worlds." Related to this lack of conceptual grounding is a third problem, i.e., the propensity to distort and caricature constructivist approaches to teaching and learning. Battista (1999), discussing constructivist approaches in mathematics education, expressed this propensity as follows:

Unfortunately, most educators (including many teachers, educational administrators, and professors of education) and almost all noneducators (including mathematicians, scientists, and writers for the popular press) have no substantive understanding of the research-based constructivist theory that I have alluded to above. Many of them conceive of constructivism as a pedagogical stance that entails a type of non rigorous, intellectual anarchy that lets student pursue whatever interest them and invent and use any mathematical methods they wish, whether these methods are correct or not. (p. 429)

Because constructivism concerns itself with the developmental appropriateness of learning, some observers (and unfortunately some practitioners) see the teacher's role as merely making classroom arrangements so that students can show what they already know. This misapprehension obviates the active role of the teacher as facilitator and "co-constructer" of knowledge with their students.

At its epistemological core, constructivism affirms that knowledge is constructed (made) rather than discovered (found); and, as such, all knowledge is inseparable from the individual learner's language, values, interests, experiences, and culture. In diametrical opposition to the tenants of philosophical realism which adheres to the facts versus values distinction or the belief in an objective world that exists outside of ourselves, constructivism holds a nonrealist position in recognition that it is impossible to "draw the line between what is outside of us and what is inside of us" (Smith, 1993, p. 9) in the "real world." To make a sharp distinction between the realist perspective of technical-rational versus the nonrealist perspective of constructivist pedagogy, constructivism recognizes, rather than attempts to ignore, human consciousness and moral autonomy.

Learning is, therefore, a meaning-making process in that new information must be mentally engaged in order to have meaning (von Glasersfeld, 1981). Contrary to the behaviorists' assumption that new information is simply added to one's storehouse of data, knowledge is constructed when the individual seeks to reconcile the disjuncture between his or her current interpretations of the world with a discordant new experience. Copple, Sigel, and Saunders (1984) refer to this mental engagement as "discrepancy resolution." In creating this resolution, the individual transforms and elaborates both new and former interpretations in accordance with his or her values or purposes. This is crucial because what makes us want to learn is our drive to make sense of ourselves and our world. In other words, learning is an inherently social and moral undertaking because humans are social and moral beings. Individuals are drawn to information that helps them resolve questions or accomplish acts that are consistent to their values. That is why, for example, teachers often report that they never fully or deeply understood a particular subject matter until they began teaching it (in a nontechnical mode) to others. Their desire to help others understand induces teachers to connect with and reconstruct information such that it makes sense for them in a way that it never had before. Conversely, teaching in a technical-rational mode actually diverts the meaning-making process and thus attempts, for the presumed sake of efficiency, to impose someone else's constructed knowledge.

To illustrate, I share the story of one teacher's transformative experience of shifting from the transmission to the constructivist model of teaching. The scene opens with Sharon, a young elementary school teacher who had been working with students who had been labeled learning disabled. On this sunny fall afternoon, Sharon sat with six students, all boys, around a table in her classroom in a newly added wing of the building. Her frustration mounted as she struggled to keep the students' attention on her carefully planned reading lesson. The boys had other ideas about how they would rather spend their time. They chatted, provoked, nudged, and poked each other. They twisted, turned, and fidgeted. Sharon, in response, did everything she could think of to capture their attention. She attempted to make the story more interesting by adding animation to her voice. She corrected, cajoled, and offered the students rewards for their attention; all to no avail.

The situation reached its crescendo when a truck bearing workmen with a load of sod pulled up outside of her window. As the men began work, laying sod on the bare ground outside of her rather large window, the boys watched in abject fascination. Sharon knew it was all over. She had lost the struggle; and, in a moment of despair that often precedes epiphany, she closed her book and directed her students to do the same. Breaking all the rules of order, plans, and schedules, she told her students to get their paper and pencils and proceeded to take them to the work site where they were to interview the men about their work. It was a last-ditch effort, and one with which she was less than comfortable; but, desperate times call for desperate measures.

Once outside, she apologized to the men for the interruption and asked, if it was not too much of an imposition, that the boys be allowed to interview them about their work. The men responded with kind enthusiasm; and, to her delight, an incredible exchange took place between the students and the workers. The boys asked impressively informed questions, ones, in fact, that would not have occurred to Sharon. The men, in turn, responded with rather sophisticated answers, which, to Sharon's complete surprise, the boys began recording on their paper. Less than a half hour later, teacher and students returned to the classroom and began writing reports on sod laying.

The students' rough drafts contained the expected array of misspellings and grammatical errors; but Sharon noted with deep satisfaction the concentration, care, and effort they exerted. In addition, it occurred to her that she had never before seen them write anything of such length and detail. Moreover, she had to admit that she had not considered them capable of doing so. As the afternoon wore on, she assisted them in consulting various reference materials as they added to their drafts. In the days that followed, Sharon used the drafts to teach grammar, dictionary, reference, and computer skills as they refined and rewrote their papers. Her greatest frustration now was how quickly time slipped by, a frustration that apparently was shared by her students who seemed annoyed at the ringing of the dismissal bell.

The students were so proud of their finished reports that Sharon arranged a presentation for the students to share them with the principal and other classes. It was during the presentation, as she looked on with a mixture of pride and admiration, that she knew that she could not return to teaching the way she once had. Everything had changed. The way she viewed her students' capabilities had changed, the contentious manner in which she and they had related to one another had changed, and everything she had believed about teaching and learning was irrevocably altered. Although she was uncertain about how she was to proceed, Sharon realized that there was now no going back

As is clear from Sharon's story, constructivist pedagogy does not involve a set of prescribed methods. Constructivism can be characterized, but it cannot under any circumstances be proceduralized. There can be no "cookbook" of procedures, because attempts to develop one would obviously signify a failure to escape the technical-rational approach incommensurately at odds with constructivist philosophy. Bluntly stated, those who ask for specific constructivist techniques are simply asking the wrong question altogether. Such a request reveals a mindset still entangled in the technical-rational framework, still searching for something outside of oneself.

Becoming a constructivist educator requires nothing short of a complete conceptual shift involving one's fundamental beliefs about the nature of teaching and learning. One must now understand that teaching comes from the inside. It is a process of intense intellectual and personal engagement. As Giroux (1993) affirmed:

> By viewing teachers as intellectuals, we can illuminate the important
> idea that all human activity involves some form of thinking. No activ-

ity, regardless of how routinized it might become, can be abstracted
from the functioning of the mind in some capacity. This is a crucial issue, because by arguing that the use of the mind is a general part of
all human activity we dignify the human capacity for integrating
thinking and practice, and in doing so highlight the core of what it
means to view teachers as reflective practitioners. (Giroux, 1993, p.
275)

Subsequently, teaching cannot be prepackaged, standardized, or scripted
because no two teaching acts are ever the same.

Toward Authentic Inclusion

What I have aspired to make apparent is this—if schools are to make
genuine progress toward authentic inclusion, fundamental changes must
take place in the instructional framework of general education classrooms
informed by the technical-rational framework. Failing to accomplish this
would only perpetuate the dilemma of returning students to classrooms
where they have no hope of flourishing. The process of achieving these
changes is no doubt a daunting prospect, one requiring not only intense conceptual and philosophical shifts, but also inevitable moral and political challenges (Gallagher, 2001).

One of the most imposing barriers to relinquishing the traditional
technical-rational framework is that it has become so deeply entrenched in
the way we see the world. The ability to envision or comprehend an alternative constructivist framework requires a conceptual shift of profound magni-
tude. For most educators, there is little in their previous experiences to help
them realize such a transformation. Almost everything in their lives serves to
reconfirm existing hegemonic forces, including teacher "training" programs
that are precisely what the term implies, programs that elevate technical
training above authentic, intellectually transformative education. What is, or
should be, apparent is that teachers cannot accord students intellectual
autonomy if they have not experienced it themselves.

In addition to the denial of intellectual autonomy, teachers are also
denied professional autonomy. Overwhelmed by the escalating political demands for maintaining standards, demonstrating accountability, delivering
mandated curricula, and implementing management programs, teachers
find themselves perpetually on the defensive. This situation contributes to
what Boyles (1998) referred to as a state of "intransitivity," or "noncritical
(in)action." This term does not imply that teachers are to blame. On the contrary, he observed that "teachers are positioned at the center of this nexus of
power and, as such, are severely constrained in an educational system that

has been shown to be inflexible and repressive of transformative ideas" (p. 178). On a more hopeful note, though, he indicated that increasing numbers of educators "are becoming more aware of the detrimental effects of intransitivity" (p. 193). However, as he further explained, this partial awareness has led to a state of "semitransitivty," meaning that, although educators are pursuing change, they are doing so in a series of unrelated segments.

I would venture that this semitransitive series of unrelated gains very clearly resonates with many current efforts to achieve inclusive education. Attempting to include special needs students into classrooms still dominated by technique-driven pedagogy, accommodations, and adaptations notwithstanding, will accomplish little at best. At worst, it will perpetuate the opposite of inclusive aims, "a system in which education becomes [is] an instrument in legitimizing and defining hierarchy; in which schools are a site where people are sorted, graded, classified and labeled, hence giving credence to the tacit social value that dignity is to be earned" (Purpel, 1993, p. 282). Even so, what can be done to transcend these obstacles?

We might begin by making teacher education a transformative experience. As it stands now, colleges of education tend to devote most of their efforts to credentialing and precious little to exposing undergraduate, or even graduate, students to the philosophical and conceptual foundations of their own profession. Instead, most graduate with little or no serious inquiry into what their work is all about (Boyles, 1998; Purpel, 1993). More to the point, they are seldom encouraged to immerse themselves deeply in the political, moral, and pedagogical critiques that might enable them to develop a decidedly sophisticated analysis to the challenges they confront as educators.

A heavy repertoire of prescriptive teaching methods, lightly sprinkled with a bit of theory around the edges, virtually consigns teachers to the role of the "proletarianized' worker Apple (1993) so aptly described. So long as teachers are taught to look outside of themselves to define the nature of their work, whatever efforts educators make toward inclusive reforms will inevitably reconfirm conventional practices with all the consequences attendant thereto. If this continues to be the case, the destiny of inclusive education will likely confirm the time-honored adage—the more things change, the more they stay the same.

References

Apple, M. W. (1982). *Education and power*. Boston and London: Routledge & Kegan Paul.

———— (1993). Controlling the work of teachers. In H. S. Shapiro, & D. E. Purpel (Eds.), *Critical social issues in American education: Toward the 21st century* (pp. 255–271). New York & London: Longman.

Battista, M. T. (1999). The mathematical miseducation of America's youth: Ignoring research and scientific study in education. *Phi Delta Kappan, 80(6)*, 425–433.

Bourdieu, P., & Passeron, J.-C. (1977). *Reproduction in education, society, and culture.* London and Beverly Hills: Sage.

Bowles, S., & Gintis, H. (1976). *Schooling in capitalist America.* New York: Basic Books.

Boyles, D. (1998). *American education and corporations: The free market goes to school.* New York and London: Garland.

Bronfenbrenner, U. (1979). *The ecology of human development.* Cambridge, MA: Harvard University Press.

Brooks, J. G., & Brooks, M. G. (1993). *In search of understanding: The case for constructivist classrooms.* Alexandria, VA: Association for Supervision and Curriculum Development.

Callahan, R. (1962). *Education and the cult of efficiency.* Chicago: University of Chicago Press.

Chapman, P. D. (1988). *Schools as sorters: Lewis M. Terman, applied psychology, and the intelligence testing movement, 1890–1930.* New York: New York University Press.

Cleverley, J., & Phillips, D. C. (1986). *Visions of childhood: Influential models from Locke to Spock* (Rev. ed.). New York: Teachers College Press.

Copple, C., Sigel, I., & Saunders, R. (1984). *Educating the young thinker.* New York: D. Van Nostrand.

Dudley-Marling, C. (1996). Curriculum-based assessment and literacy instruction: A political critique. In W. Stainback & S. Stainback (Eds.), *Controversial Issues Confronting Special Education: Divergent Perspectives* (2nd ed.). Needham Heights, MA: Allyn & Bacon.

Gallagher, D. J. (1998). The scientific knowledge base of special education: Do we know what we think we know? *Exceptional Children, 64(4)*, 493–502.

———— (2001). Neutrality as a moral standpoint, conceptual confusion, and the full inclusion debate. *Disability and Society, 16(5)*, 637–654.

Giddens, A. (1993). *New rules of the sociological method: A positive critique of interpretive sociologies* (2nd ed.). Stanford, CA: Stanford University Press.

Giroux, H. A. (1993). Teachers as transformative intellectuals. In H. S. Shapiro, & D. E. Purpel (Eds.), *Critical social issues in American education: Toward the 21st century* (pp. 85–102). New York and London: Longman.

Hacking, I. (1990). *The taming of chance.* Cambridge, UK: Cambridge University Press.

Heshusius, L. (1984). Why would they and I want to do it? A phenomenological-theoretical view of special education. *Learning Disabilities Quarterly, 7,* 363–367.

Hodkinson, P. (1997). Neo-Fordism and teacher professionalism. *Teacher Development, 3(1)*, 69–81.

Hunter, M. C. (1986). Mastery teaching. El Segundo, CA: TIP Publications.

Iano, R. P. (2003). Inside the schools: Special education and inclusion reform. In D. J. Gallagher, L. Heshusius, R. P. Iano, & T. Skrtic, *Challenging orthodoxy in special education: Dissenting voices.* Denver, CO: Love Publishing.

———— (1990). Special education teachers: Technicians or educators? *Journal of Learning Disabilities, 23,* 462–465.

Kauffman, J. M. (1995). Why we must celebrate a diversity of restrictive environments. *Learning Disabilities Research & Practice, 10(4),* 225–232.

Kavale, K. A. (2000). *Inclusion: Rhetoric and reality surrounding the integration of students with disabilities.* The Iowa Academy of Education: Occasional Research Paper #2. Des Moines, IA: FINE Foundation.

MacKenzie, D. (1981). *Statistics in Great Britain: 1865–1930: The social construction of scientific knowledge.* Edinburgh: Edinburgh University Press.

MacMillan, D. L., Gresham, F. M., & Forness, S. R. (1996). Full-inclusion: An empirical perspective. *Behavioral Disorders, 21(2),* 145–159.

Piaget, J. (1970). *Structuralism.* New York: Basic Books.

Poplin, M. S. (1988). The reductionistic fallacy in learning disabilities: Replicating the past by reducing the present. *Journal of Learning Disabilities, 21(7),* 389–400.

Purpel, D. E. (1993). Educational discourse and global crisis: What's a teacher to do? In H. S. Shapiro, & D.E. Purpel (Eds.), *Critical social issues in American education: Toward the 21st century* (pp. 85–102). New York and London: Longman.

Robinson, D. N. (1981). *An intellectual history of psychology.* New York: Macmillan.

Sapon-Shevin, M. (1996). Full inclusion as a disclosing tablet: Revealing the flaws in our present system. *Theory Into Practice, 35(1),* 35–41.

Singham, M. (1998). The canary in the mine: The achievement gap between black and white students. *Phi Delta Kappan, 80,* 9–15.

Skinner, B. F. (1983). *A matter of consequences: Part three of an autobiography.* New York: Knopf: Distributed by Random House.

Skrtic, T. M. (1991a). *Behind special education: A critical analysis of professional knowledge and school organization.* Denver, CO: Love Publishing.

———— (1991b). The special education paradox: Equity as a way to excellence. *Harvard Educational Review, 61(2),* 148–206.

Smith, J. K. (1989). *The nature of social and educational inquiry: Empiricism versus interpretation.* Norwood, NJ: Ablex.

———— (1993). *After the demise of empiricism: The problem of judging social and educational inquiry.* Norwood, NJ: Ablex.

Spring, J. (1989). *The sorting machine revisited: National educational policy since 1945* (Rev. ed.). New York and London: Longman.

SRA Direct Instruction. DeSoto, TX: SRA/McGraw-Hill.

Success for All Foundation. Baltimore, MD. http://www.successforall.net

Taylor, M. D. (1976). *Roll of thunder, hear my cry.* New York: Dial Press.

Thorndike, Edward L. (1910). The contribution of psychology to education. *The Journal of Educational Psychology, 1,* 5–12.

von Glasersfeld, E. (1981). The concepts of adaptation and viability in a radical constructivist theory of knowledge. In I. E. Sigel, D. M. Brodinsky, & R. M. Golinkoff (Eds.), *New directions in Piagetian theory and practice.* Hillsdale, NJ: Lawrence Erlbaum.

Watson, J. B. (1913). Psychology as the behaviorist views it. *Psychological Review, 20,* 158–177.

———— (1924). *Behaviorism.* New York: The People's Institute Publishing Company.

10 Transforming Literacy Instruction: Unpacking the Pedagogy of Privilege

Susan Peters

> I feel that people shouldn't label other people, because they don't like to be labeled themselves.... If you found out what they're not good at and put a label on them they would feel real low because you are messing around with their weakness.... I think that it is about time someone told them that there is no difference between us.
>
> Maenzanise, "How It Feels to Be Labeled"

This chapter marks the third time I have put pen to paper to engage readers in what I consider to be the most influential experience of my thirty-year professional career as a teacher-educator. The interactions I had with forty African American high school youths labeled as learning disabled have become deeply embedded in my pedagogical approach to teaching and are seared in my memory as if the experiences occurred only yesterday instead of ten plus years ago. In fact, these students' voices color everything I do as a teacher today.

The first time I wrote about my experiences with these students (Peters, Klein, & Shadwick, 1998), I focused on what the students taught me about themselves through their written and oral discourses. The second time, I focused on the learning process, or "how to" develop literacy skills (Peters, 1999). This time, I turn the spotlight on myself and my profession, to examine the teaching process. In the following sections I first introduce the approach I used in teaching literacy to these students. I then give a description of the experiences themselves, with little analytical commentary. In the final section, I analyze myself and the approach I used, provide some reflections on the lessons I have learned, and propose some ways that these lessons might be helpful for teacher-educators.

Before I begin, I have three confessions to make. First, I am not formally trained in literacy instruction (unless one counts an undergraduate degree in English literature). Second, my "disability" is very visible and "severe"—according to U.S. federal legislative guidelines. This so-called "objective" reality is integral to the subjective realities I bring to my teaching, and I will reflect on these as I talk about my experiences. Third, when I interacted with the youths on this literacy project, I was only dimly aware of Paulo Freire's influence on my approaches to teaching. It was only in reflection that I came to understand his influence and the ways I had appropriated his principles of critical pedagogy—not only in my beliefs about teaching, but in my daily practical applications to classroom instruction.

Literacy Instruction and Paulo Freire's Critical Pedagogy

Literacy is arguably a key curriculum component to successful academic achievement of diverse learners, and in particular, students labeled as learning disabled. The current system of education too often shunts students who do not conform off to special classes where their literacy instruction amounts to learning required rules of conformity embedded within a language and discourse of deviance and deficiency that results in alienation and worsens the literacy problem and may trigger school failure. Specifically, "disabled" students are relegated "to a silent and *silenced* world where they become what they are perceived as being: incapable, illiterate, dysfunctional and non-productive members of school and society" (Peters, 1999, p. 104).

A small but growing number of educators in North America have begun to apply a Freirian approach to literacy instruction with various minority and "disadvantaged" students who have been silenced by traditional methods (Shor, 1987). I have re-created Freire's approach by applying the central tenets of disability studies to this literacy instruction with students labeled as learning disabled. Specifically, this approach views disability within historical, political, and social contexts of teaching and learning, rather than as an innate individual trait that needs fixing. Based on a critical pedagogy that combines theory with practice, the goal of this pedagogy is to form a new educational praxis of transformation and liberation from oppression that enables students labeled as disabled to find their own voice, to rediscover a positive identity, and to gain literacy skills through empowerment and self-discovery.

This praxis has two stages. First, individuals labeled as disabled unveil the world of oppression, and through praxis, commit themselves to its transformation. In the second stage, the reality of oppression is transformed, resulting in an educational pedagogy that ceases to belong to the oppressor (in this case the literacy instruction of students with learning disabilities) but becomes a pedagogy belonging to the students in an ongoing process of liberation from oppression. Ultimately, this alternative to traditional literacy instruction seeks to elevate the learners to a status of teacher-educator in their own right, and in the process, transforms the curriculum and teaching.

Paulo Freire first developed and applied critical pedagogy in his work with illiterate peasants in Brazil in the late 1960s and 1970s. At the heart of his approach is the concept of conscientization (or *conscientização* in the original Portuguese). *Conscientização* is literally "learning to perceive social, political, and economic contradictions, and to take action against the oppressive elements of reality" (Freire, 1993, p. 19).

Conscientization involves a process of becoming aware of oppressive political, economic, and cultural systems (not the least of which are schools and formal schooling), and then uses this awareness to transform self and society. Conscientization and critical pedagogy are committed to reflection and action. This approach has historical and theoretical links to Jürgen Habermas's (1987) concept of communicative action and to John Dewey's (1938) educational pragmatism, with its emphasis on problem-solving and question-posing within the context of teaching and learning in schools.

I witnessed conscientization in action in Southern Africa in the late 1980s as a participant-observer in grassroots disability rights initiatives. Specifically, disabled Zimbabweans appropriated conscientization to educate themselves and society in their liberation movement for social justice and equal rights. Their approach was modeled after the black majority in that country, who took up arms to fight the apartheid system and to gain their freedom and independence. According to Mupindu, a black disabled Zimbabwean, "the approach to the war of independence and subsequently to the founding of the disability movement in Zimbabwe was to conscientize the community so that they understood the source of their sufferings: the oppressive discrimination system" (Peters & Chimedza, 2000, p. 254). This conscientization was accomplished during the Zimbabwean war of liberation through "pungwes," or meetings between the guerrillas and the people in which they discussed their plight and actions they might take against discrimination. Conscientization in the disabled people's movement in Zimbabwe took place in much the same way. They met together in groups to discuss their marginalized status and to strategize ways to change the situation.

Assumptions of Conscientization

This conscientization process, when applied to the context of education in schools, rests on five basic assumptions:

1. Education is an act of love and courage. It is not paternalistic, but promotes self-discovery and self-worth. It carries the courage of convictions contained in a "radical" education involving commitment to one's values. "It is predominantly critical, loving, humble, communicative, and therefore a positive stance" (Freire, 1973, p. 10).

2. Education is political. Curriculum and instruction are political processes. Many special educators cloak their standardized assessments, medical labels, and mandated referral procedures in "objective" terms. However, the process of becoming learning disabled is, in fact, a political act (Peters, 1996). For example, students who do not conform to the norms of classroom instruction are diagnosed and labeled as if their nonconformity is not socially constructed, but an innate personal characteristic. Once a student has been labeled, the content of the curriculum is also politically constructed around remediating deficiencies in the learner, as if the environment has no influence on learning. As Freire asserts, "One teaches how to think through teaching of content. Neither can we teach content by itself as if the school context in which this content is treated could be reduced to a neutral space where social conflicts would not manifest themselves" (Freire, 1993, p. 24).

3. Literacy, language, comprehension, and communication are inseparably linked to power and ideology. This link is very apparent in special education, where the label traditionally has become the person. Decisions and actions in special education derive from the language used to describe a person who is considered disabled. The language used within this discipline communicates a medicalization of disability that is all-powerful, with oppressive consequences (Peters, 1999).

4. Education must be grounded in students' worldviews. We must begin by respecting the values, knowledge, and language of students. Many students with learning difficulties in written language have strengths in oral language, as well as untapped knowledge and values that they can bring to literacy learning. The awakening of a critical consciousness through teaching to this strength leads students to become politicized and aware of the context within which they learn, culminating in new forms of expression.

5. Education involves a dialectical relationship between reflection and action, or what is called praxis. "Nobody becomes an educator on Tuesday at four in the afternoon" (Freire, 1973, p. 56). Students as well as teachers continuously develop their literacy skills through reflection on practice, followed by action, which in turn leads to further reflection.

When I began my literacy instruction with the African American youths in an urban high school in the Midwest of the United States, I had come fresh from my experiences in Zimbabwe. At a deep level, I had internalized the assumptions and appropriated the critical pedagogy of conscientization to a greater extent than I realized at the time.

The Literacy Project

Translated into practice, Freire's critical pedagogy has five phases. These phases constitute an approach to discourse that is characteristically generative, dynamic, progressive, and evolutionary. The act of literacy instruction is inseparable from the political act of knowing. That is, knowledge is generated through tapping into the students' productive experiences and capabilities, and they are inherently critical and reflective. The effect is that the process opens up spaces for individuals to act.

In this section, I use these phases as an analytical framework to describe the process of literacy instruction that I engaged in with the African American high school students labeled as learning disabled.

Phase 1: Educators "tune in" to the vocabulary and worldview of the students.

As a white female from a white-collar social class background, I had a lot of work to do with this group of mostly males of blue-collar social class backgrounds, to establish trust and authenticity. I began by asking them what they wanted and what they felt they were missing in their curriculum and instruction. Their answers startled me. Students stated their request starkly and succinctly: "Some teachers have that learning class. Why not teach us like regular teachers teach them even if it takes us longer if it has to. As long as we learn like they are learning, because we want to learn too." From this knowledge of their desires, I asked them why they thought they were excluded from "that learning class." Their responses were again very revealing. Virtually all 40 youths had been labeled as learning disabled at an early age—first, second, or third grade—because, in their words, they had missed a lot of school and gotten behind, or they "acted out" and their teachers did not want them in class. They related stories of being called Loco-Dummies (the epithet for LD) and "head-bangers." They had rejected these epithets for the most part, despite the odds, and exhibited an inner resiliency that I discovered was one of their greatest untapped strengths. So we began our journey together, exploring the meaning of their experiences through dialogue, and eventually written word.

Phase 2: Learners search for generative words at two levels: syllable richness and high experiential meaning.

From the very beginning, students expressed a need to go beyond their "three-letter spelling words." So, together, we searched for words with the syllabic richness that they craved. They appropriated the pedagogy of privilege to their own ends, learning the vocabulary of their oppressors to describe their experiences and to turn the tables. To begin, students expressed their experiences of instruction: "They [teachers] talk all day, but you still don't know what to do, so you want to go to sleep on them and they get mad. But how can I stay awake with someone that I don't know what they're talking about?" A search of words in *Webster's Dictionary* turned up the word *pedantic* which the students appropriated as an apt description of their experience: "One who makes a display of learning either in ostentation or in unduly emphasizing minutiae." In the same way, teachers who "just talk as if they're selling our parents this product but not going through with the job" became characterized as arbitrary, aloof, and uncaring. Low expectations became a "predicament" to be challenged, gossip became "false accusations" and "never being able to do anything" (no dances and only one pep rally a year) became deprivation of their rights. Armed with this new vocabulary derived from their experiences, students began to provide rich visual images of their experiences through writing.

Phase 3: Learners codify these generative words into visual images that stimulate them to emerge as conscious makers of their own culture.

Students codified (in their words, "grouped") their generative words to describe what school looks like, what actions take place in school, and how it feels. They went on to expand these codified words into short snapshot descriptions of their school. They shared these snapshots with each other and through dialogue, gave each other feedback, refined, and expanded their images.

> What It's Like [at our high school]
>   spirited
>   great losses—deprivation
>   maze
>   crowded intersections

green halls
cages—harsh, arbitrary, uncaring
big—humongous, enormous
phony—chatty, pedantic
fashion show—flashy, ostentatious

What We Do
learn—gain knowledge
train—self-discipline
run down the hall
sleep
yell
talk back
litter
fight—altercation, harassment
curse teachers
sit in boring classes
gossip—malicious rumor
sleep—rest, day-dream
pass judgments—false accusations

How We Feel
pride
like crying
excited
ready to get out
tired of the same people
aloof principal
apart, separate
pessimistic
opinionated
frustrated
smart
dumb
embarrassed
nervous
shy

Expanded into a snapshot, one student wrote:

"Our high school is a big enormous school. We have a lot of people who like to gossip about people, and at other times they have false accusations to make about some people, when already most people have the most pessimistic side of things."

In this phase, students chose their own forms of written expression (e.g., short essay, poetry, rap), and produced several drafts of their work. They shared their work in progress with their peers, discussed shared meanings, and revised until they were satisfied with the results.

Phase 4: Decodification takes place through dialogue with students/educators who are no longer passive recipients of knowledge.

At this stage, I shared my own writing with them, reading from excerpts of an essay on labeling and what it meant to me as a disabled person. In response, one student wrote an essay entitled "Can't Miss Reality." He opened with these thoughts:

> What you wrote about really existed. That's when reality really hit me because I thought I was the only person who felt different.... Now I know that I'm not the only student who feels what I feel. I have problems. Some of my predicaments or low expectations are when people put me down, or when at times I get low self-esteem and let other people put me down, but I come to reality and say, "Mashingaidze, ain't nobody perfect. You're learning like everybody else." Everyone has problems and alter-egos to maintain. And mine is to succeed in life and not let anyone else be pulling me down." (Mashingaidze is a literary name chosen by this student. It means "Complex Person" in the Shona language.)

Another student wrote an essay about "How It Feels to Be Labeled":

> I feel that people shouldn't label other people, because they don't like to be labeled themselves. If more people would think about how it feels to be called a name or put in categories, they would know how it feels to be called a name. I think that it is about time someone told them that there is no difference between us.

> If you found out what they're not good at and put a label on them, they would feel real low because you are messing around with their weakness. And no one wants you to play with their weakness because if it is your weakness you can say too much about it.

Phase 5: Creative codification explicitly aimed at action. Students reject their passive role as objects and become active subjects transforming the world around them.

The students' exploration of the experience of "being LD" led them naturally to a desire for change. At this stage, they were writing in earnest for a purpose of their own choosing—an underground newsletter whose audience would be teachers and students at their school. Their chosen title for this newsletter was "From Our View." In this newsletter, they arrived at a slate of recommendations: more freedom, school spirit, more say in decisions that affected them, and a challenge to teachers: "Teachers need to take time out to discuss the class work. We need to understand more about our work." In its first year, we published several editions of the newsletter. I continue to publish editions each year for the students in the university courses I teach. University students, in their course evaluations, consistently comment on the power of these students' voices in terms of challenging their beliefs and practices.

Students in the literacy project also actively responded to the epithets they had been given and decided to choose "pen names" from an African language (Shona) that exemplified their newfound sense of pride and self-identity. Marcus became Hazvizikamwi, The Caring One; Toya became Mashingaidze, The Complex Person; Greg became Mandivamba, The Practical No-Nonsense-One; Monica became Dekesai, The Laughing One.

A Critical-Reflective Analysis of the Literacy Project

The above description of my re-creation of Freire's approach to literacy instruction is, of course, much more than a literacy project. At its heart, the project is a process of conscientization that rests on the ideals of a radical democracy. These ideals uncover and challenge the politics of social inequality and the oppressive identity politics inherent in school systems where beliefs and practices dehumanize the bodies, demoralize the minds, and silence the voices of a large number of our youths in U.S. schools.

My part in this process of conscientization was an eminently political act in its own right. I make this statement with no apologies, but rather with pride. To me, the content of the curriculum in schools carries a political message and frames the dialogue. As one student put it, it is about time we turned the tables. My teaching as a political act represents a counter-hegemonic discourse for critical reflection. Specifically, "Schools are sites of constant political and cultural struggle" (Anderson, 1998, p. 591).

My own life as an educator has been a constant daily struggle against discrimination and disrespect. Two incidents at the university level of public schooling stand out as exemplars of this struggle. First, upon my arrival as a newly hired assistant professor, I discovered there were no accessible toilet facilities in my building. To alleviate this problem, a professor organized a bake-sale charity campaign set up in the main lobby to raise money for installation of an accessible toilet. I immediately dismantled the site and derailed the campaign.

Second, as a core member of the African Studies faculty at my university, I was essentially barred from active participation due to the fact that meetings were held on the second floor of a building with no elevator. Appeals to the director to relocate the meetings met with active resistance. The director had dedicated years to dismantling apartheid and separate facilities in South Africa but failed to make the philosophical connection with my inability to attend African Studies meetings. An elevator was installed in the building, only after two years' of persistence and appeals to higher authorities.

These two examples are symbols of the culture of charity and the politics of disablement that I face in my life on a daily basis. My struggles to change attitudes and the correlational objective conditions of oppression have forged my classroom instruction, just as steel is forged from base metals. Both are complicated processes and reinforce Freire's assertion that "nobody becomes an educator on Tuesday at four in the afternoon."

Carrying these experiences with me into my classroom experiences with African American youths labeled as learning disabled, I believed my role was to help these students analyze how their subjectivities had been ideologically formed within the exploitative forces and relations of public schooling as a "ritual performance" of exclusion and dehumanization. However, as McLaren has said, Freire's approach to pedagogy "exhibits a singular awareness that the oppressed will not recognize their oppression simply because somebody has pointed it out to them. They will come to recognize their oppression through their own daily experience of struggling to survive. Struggle and critical reflection are thus dialectically related" (McLaren, 2000, p. 8). This recognition of oppression is powerfully exemplified in the student's essay "Can't Miss Reality" when he wrote "What you wrote about really exist(s). That's when reality really hit me because I thought I was the only person who felt different."

That moment of revelation on the part of the student, along with his existential questions such as "Why can't we be in that learning class?" have sustained me throughout my subsequent years of teaching and have given me the courage to put into action another student's challenge which I quoted at the beginning of this chapter: "I think it is about time someone told them [that learning class] that there is no difference between us."

For Freire, "critical pedagogy has as much to do with the teachable heart as the teachable mind and as much to do with efforts to change the world as it does with rethinking the categories [such as Learning Disabilities] that we use to analyze our current condition within history" (McLaren, 2000, p. 10). Upon critical reflection, the first basic assumption of the conscientization process—education is an act of love and courage—is a two-way street. The literacy project taught me that opening up spaces for authentic dialogue reveals the source of education as an act of love and courage. The students' love and courage sustains me as an educator.

Lessons for Educators: Making Sense of Student Voices Through a Pedagogy of Caring

In his provocative book, *Schooling as a Ritual Performance* (1986), Peter McLaren challenges all of us who "come to school" to recognize the modus operandi of the pedagogical encounter in schools as a ritual performance that carries cultural codes and symbolic action. These codes and actions are shaped by powerful organizational mandates that seek to proscribe and manipulate all aspects of performance in schools, for both teachers and students. These mandates rest on proscribed standards of behavior and their determinants and as such represent a powerful hegemonic pedagogy of privilege. Those who resist this pedagogy of privilege present an alternative of connecting action to sense making. This combination of action and reflection is the core of a critical theory of emancipation and correlates with the critical literacy instruction described in my classroom. This critical theory is necessary in order to move beyond the reductionism that plagues traditional schooling, particularly for students labeled as disabled.

In my discussion of my approach to literacy section adapted from Freire's critical pedagogy, I described the ways in which students codified and transformed their images of self and society through a pedagogy of critical literacy. Their writing is so powerful because it turns the gaze from themselves to the professionals who are ascribed as their teachers. This gaze is deeply critical of the pedantic, ostentatious, and ritual displays of teaching and learning in schools such as theirs. Using the students' gaze, I now turn to a macro-level analysis of the teaching profession, developing a view of the academy and its ideology that is grounded in their worldview. I use the same five phases of Freire's critical literacy to propose some lessons for educators.

Phase 1: Educators "tune in" to the students' vocabulary and worldview of their teachers, learning what it feels like to be labeled, segregated, and receive "needed" remedial instruction.

The organizational and legal mandates of schools have labeled students as mentally impaired, emotionally disturbed, and physically handicapped. The students in this literacy project compel us, through their voices, to "think about how it feels to be called a name or put in categories." How would it feel to label ourselves, assess our own potential for achievement, and evaluate our own progress towards our maximum potential as enablers of people who have much to contribute to our society. It may be argued that there are currently three categories of education professionals: moralists, rationalists, and pragmatists. Proper labels might be morally impaired, rationally disturbed, and pragmatically handicapped. The morally impaired argue that students with disabilities belong in pull-out programs where educators can "monitor their progress" and "protect" them from societal mistreatment. The rationally disturbed continue to assess progress or lack of progress ad nauseam while students with disabilities await placement decisions in limbo. The pragmatically handicapped credo can be capsulated in the rallying cry, "We're not ready yet. We haven't been adequately trained." Even so, students are ready. They ask, "Why not teach us like regular teachers teach them [their non-labeled and non-segregated peers]?" There are many other students like this one, and they are not waiting for the pragmatists, moralists, and rationalists to decide when we might be ready for them.

Students have pinpointed our weaknesses as educators. We are too often pedantic, arbitrary, and uncaring. Their voices impel us to critically examine our own practice and potentials, including the language and pedagogical strategies that we use. As educators, we need to conscientize ourselves, and through this conscientization, transform our practice to one that is caring and rich in experiential learning, and that builds on strengths rather than focusing on deficits.

Phases 2 & 3: Educators begin to formulate a new worldview, with new vocabulary for at-risk, learning disabled students that is rich in high experiential meaning.

In my research and reflection on the experiences of the students in this literacy project, I codified their discourse and written word. An examination of the patterns of their responses to the "problem" of disability in their lives revealed three powerful metaphors. First, these students' sense-making revealed individuals who were streetwise philosophers. These students' philosophy uncovers and challenges the gaze of professionals who too often view them as behavior problems or slow learners. Their views of these misperceptions make them angry, and they feel a deep sense of injustice: "It's just not right because I think that the next person is no better than me." Another student observed, "Labeling makes you one of two things: weak or strong. On the one hand, you get people calling you names every day. But it's an advantage because it makes you strong and able to withstand a lot of stuff from people."

However, some students are not strong enough to withstand this constant assault on their identity. Sekesai composed a rap song to express her struggle:

> BEAT UP
> There are some people
> that just beat you any kind of way,
> no matter who you are
> or what classes you are in.
> There are those who think that they're better than you
> and those who treat you special
> and those who think
> you can't do anything right.

These experiences compel us to turn the gaze on ourselves as educators. If we view ourselves as part of the (behavior) problem, we can begin to unpack the pedagogy of privilege that we perpetuate through our language and labeling practices in schools.

Second, the students' writing revealed strong image-making skills. Handling the consequences of being labeled "LD" became a juggling act. They spent a lot of energy hiding their label and keeping the secret of their special education status. Class schedules also had to be juggled. Negotiating the gatekeeping maze at the high school level is a full-time occupation. Students can get further and further behind in accumulating course credits for graduation when they are forced to take both special education and regular education subjects (e.g., math, English, language arts, and so forth), in addition to certain prerequisites. These experiences reveal a need to critically examine the consequences of labeling. Change will require a radical restructuring of schools and elimination of segregated, "pull-out" programs.

Third, students' reflections about being singled out and provided with remedial instruction are characteristic of musical rhythms and genres. For many of these students, school seems like a dirge or a march, with the same beat—repetitive and slow. As one student put it, "Some teachers have us learning out of the same book year after year, then we never have the time to learn that much out of a regular book." In their literary acts of transgression, they became jazz improvizationists, demanding solo performances and a faster tempo: "Do teachers think it is right for you to have your learning cut short? For example, who put three letter words on the board? Students know those words. Why not give us more learning things?" Students are urging educators to create schools that are characteristic of a jazz session: creative, challenging, spiritual, and harmonized.

Phases 4 & 5: Decodification and transformation aimed at action takes place.

Overall, these symbols (philosophers, image-makers, and jazz improvisationists) as metaphors of a new vision of schooling help educators understand the barriers of a pedagogy of privilege that is cloaked in a language of deficiency and failure, and in segregation practices. The alternative that students demand is a critical pedagogy of emancipation. Examining how students codify and transcend this pedagogy of privilege provides us with alternative symbols, and reveals the strengths they bring to the school context. These strengths need to be recognized and capitalized on to enhance their status as active learners with knowledge, values, and abilities that deserve respect.

The Accelerated Schools Project in the United States is one example of a school reform effort that has begun to decodify and transform past practice through building on these strengths. Educators in Accelerated Schools treat all students as if they are gifted and talented and accelerate their learning rather than remedy. These schools, with high numbers of "at-risk" students, have demonstrated high levels of achievement on a wide range of school effectiveness measures (see Finnan et al., 1996).

In "Some musings on what can be done" Henry Levin (1998) reflects that we have two choices as educators. We can accept the standards, narrow assessment criteria, and teacher-proof curriculum packages based on these criteria, or we can reject and resist by advocating for students and by inspiring them through enriched activities that build on students' strengths and life experiences. "All of this requires taking tremendous risks, including the charge of being 'out-of-compliance' with school regulations and decisions" (Levin, 1998, p. 164). Educators who take these risks embody the principle of education as an act of love and courage. This recognition of education as an act of love and courage leads us to decisions and actions that carry the potential to resist the hegemonic political context of teaching and learning, culminating in new forms of expression.

Final Reflections

Conscientization and critical pedagogy have their historical roots in acts of rebellion on the part of Brazilian peasants and Zimbabwean freedom fighters and disabled activists. The contemporary experiences of students labeled as learning disabled described in this article are not unlike the colonial imperialism experienced in these countries of the South. In his book, *The Invention of Africa: Gnosis, Philosophy and the Order of Knowledge,* V. Y. Mudimbe (1988) argues that colonial imperialism is at its most repressive in the colonization of the mind. This colonization is what led Nelson Mandela to reflect that even his thoughts are contained within the language of the oppressor. For Mudimbe, the way out of oppression is through gnosis, or seeking to know, investigating, becoming acquainted with the self. The process of gnosis is conscientization. Students labeled as learning disabled have been colonized intellectually to accept their label and the characteristics inherent in it: incapable, illiterate, dysfunctional, and nonproductive. However, as I have demonstrated, and as Mairian Corker notes in her chapter in this book, students are competent social actors who construct their own identities. Teachers, as educators, must enable and support students in this construction. Students' identity should not have to be "beat up" by the culture of labeling in schools, and their literacy skills need not be suppressed by the consequences of this culture.

Finally, Freire's approach to critical literacy has been criticized by Ellsworth (1989) and others. These critics argue that Freire ignores unequal power relations that are inherent in the roles of students and teachers. Specifically, Ellsworth asserts that critical pedagogy rests on the "Utopian" ideal that "all ideas are tolerated and subjected to rational critical assessment against fundamental judgments and moral principles" (p. 314). Correlated to this argument, my research and teaching practice have often been subjected to the criticism that my disability makes my work biased, nonrational, and subjective. These criticisms lack the self-reflective knowledge that the "able-bodied" world contains its own biases and unequal power relations, and further, that these biases represent a hegemonic ideology that is pervasive in schools and the academy. I argue that it is time to turn the tables and to begin to unpack this pedagogical discourse of privilege. This work of unpacking the medicalized world of disability can lead to powerful reconceptualizations, such as Mashingaidze's insights in his essay, "Can't Miss Reality."

In a speech to a packed audience of professional educators, I challenged my peers to begin this work of unpacking our baggage. I called myself a social constructivist (as opposed to a moralist, pragmatist, or rational-ist). It is a category that contains a low incidence population of educators, but I'd like to see it grow. A social constructivist believes there are multiple realities and multiple subjectivities. Where these realities are distorted by misplaced altruism and benevolent humanitariansim, the social constructiv-ist works to change perceptions, to provide new paradigms. This work re-quires that labels be destroyed (including those I have used to illustrate my points) and that segregated classrooms be relegated to times past. The key dialectical elements of conscientization, praxis, and self-discovery contained in a Pedagogy of Caring—that is essentially a political act of love and cour-age—must become central to transforming educational practice. This trans-formation is the work of the coming decades.

References

Anderson, G. L. (1998). Toward authentic participation: Deconstructing the dis-courses of participatory reforms in education. *American Educational Research Journal, 35(4)*, 571–603.

Dewey, J. (1938). *Experience and education*. London: Macmillan.

Ellsworth, E. (1989). Why doesn't this feel empowering? Working through the repres-sive myths of critical pedagogy. *Harvard Educational Review, 59(3)*, 297–324.

Finnan, C., St. John, E. P., McCarthy, J., & Slovacek, S. P. (1996). *Accelerated schools in Action: Lessons from the field*. Thousand Oaks, CA: Corwin Press.

Freire, P. (1973). *Education for critical consciousness*. New York: Continuum.

———— (1993). *Pedagogy of the oppressed* (M. Bergman Ramos, Trans.). New York: Con-tinuum.

Habermas, J. (1987). *The theory of communicative action*. Boston: Beacon, 1987.

Levin, H. M. (1998). Some musings on what can be done. In B. Franklin (Ed.), *When children don't learn: Student failure and the culture of teaching* (pp. 160–173). New York: Teachers College Press.

McLaren, P. (1986). *Schooling as a ritual performance: Towards a political economy of edu-cational symbols and gestures*. London & New York: Routledge.

———— (2000). Paulo Freire's Pedagogy of Possibility. In S. Steiner, H. M. Frank, P. McLaren, & R. E. Bahruth (Eds.), *Freirian pedagogy, praxis, and possibilities: Pro-jects for the new millennium* (pp. 1–22). New York: Falmer.

Mudimbe, V. Y. (1988). *The invention of Africa: Gnosis, philosophy, and the order of knowl-edge*. Bloomington: Indiana University Press.

Peters, S. J. (1996). The politics of disability identity. In L. Barton (Ed.), *Disability and society: Emerging issues and insights* (pp. 215–234). Essex, England: Addison Wesley Longman Ltd.

———— (1999). Transforming disability identity through critical literacy and the cultural politics of language. In M. Corker & S. French (Eds.), *Disability discourse* (pp. 103–115). Buckingham and Philadelphia: Open University Press.

Peters, S. J., & Chimedza, R. (2000). Conscientization and the cultural politics of education: A radical minority perspective. *Comparative Education Review, 44(3),* 245–271.

Peters, S. J., Klein, A., & Shadwick, C. (1998). From our voices: Special education and the "alter-eagle" problem. In B. Franklin (Ed.), *When children don't learn: Student failure and the culture of teaching* (pp. 99–115). New York: Teachers College Press.

Shor, I. (1987). *Freire for the classroom: A sourcebook for liberatory teaching.* Portsmouth, NH: Boynton/Cook Publishers.

Contributors

Julie Allan, PhD, is a professor at the University of Stirling in the United Kingdom (j.e.allan@stir.ac.uk).

Ellen Brantlinger, EdD, is an emeritus professor at Indiana University in Bloomington, Indiana. (brantlin@indiana.edu).

Scot Danforth, PhD, is an associate professor at the University of Missouri-St. Louis in St. Louis, Missouri. (scot@umsl.edu).

Nirmala Erevelles, PhD, is an associate professor at the University of Alabama in Tusscaloosa, Alabama. (nerevell@bamaed.ua.edu).

Susan Gabel, PhD, is a professor at National-Louis University in Chicago, Illinois,. (sgabel@nl.edu).

Deborah Gallagher, PhD, is a professor at the University of Northern Iowa, Cedar Falls, Iowa. (deborah.gallagher@uni.edu).

Anne Ruggles Gere, PhD, is a professor at the University of Michigan in Ann Arbor, Michigan. (argere@umich.edu).

Susan Peters, PhD, is an associate professor at Michigan State University in East Lansing, Michigan. (speters@msu.edu).

Linda Ware, PhD, is an associate professor at City University of New York in New York. (lware@ccny.cuny.cdu).

Subject Index

Author Index

Disability Studies in Education

GENERAL EDITORS: SUSAN L. GABEL & SCOT DANFORTH

The book series Disability Studies in Education is dedicated to the publication of monographs and edited volumes that integrate the perspectives, methods, and theories of disability studies with the study of issues and problems of education. The series features books that further define, elaborate upon, and extend knowledge in the field of disability studies in education. Special emphasis is given to work that poses solutions to important problems facing contemporary educational theory, policy, and practice.

To order other books in this series, please contact our Customer Service Department:

(800) 770-LANG (within the U.S.)
(212) 647-7706 (outside the U.S.)
(212) 647-7707 FAX

Or browse by series:

WWW.PETERLANGUSA.COM